The Quotable Sailor

Books by Christopher Caswell

Smarter Charters
Megayachts 2000
The Basic Book of Boating
Championship Dinghy Racing

The Quotable
Sailor

EDITED BY
CHRISTOPHER CASWELL

THE LYONS PRESS
Guilford, Connecticut
An imprint of The Globe Pequot Press

The Lyons Press is an imprint of the Globe Pequot Press.

Printed in United States of America

10 9 8 7 6 5 4 3 2 1

Design by Compset, Inc.

The Library of Congress Cataloging-in-Publication Data.
The quotable sailor / edited by Christopher Caswell.
    p. cm.
   Includes bibliographical references and index.
   ISBN 1-58574-166-3
    1. Sailing—Quotations, maxims, etc.   I. Caswell, Christopher.

PN6084.S26 Q68 2001
797.1'24—dc21

                                          2001029151

For my father, who shared with me his passion for the sea and his love for reading, both of which led to this book. Thanks for being a great crew all these years, Dad!

Contents

Introduction

My mother loved aphorisms—those short one-liners that manage to summarize a concept or philosophy in just a few words, and she collected them like most people would stamps or baseball cards. As a child, I can remember being fascinated by her bulletin board, on which were thumb-tacked clippings and scraps of torn paper with scrawled phrases that covered every aspect of life, and she passed that enthusiasm along to me.

I don't remember many of them, although I'm sure that they remain in a shoebox somewhere for me to find one of these days, and they leaned heavily toward justifying or explaining our sometimes bohemian lifestyle, such as "No one ever died from an unmade bed."

As a young sailor, I was also an insatiable reader about sailing and I started keeping little notebooks in which I would jot down quotable nuggets of wisdom about sailing. Some were acquired from books, many were passed along by other sailors, but all were perhaps as close as sailors get to haiku, the deceptively simple Japanese poetry where less is more.

As the editor of *Sea* magazine, many of these found their way on to my own office bulletin board as well as later as the senior editor of *Yachting*. So I had a wealth of quotations to start with, and I've had a lovely time going through my fairly extensive sailing library as well as canvassing bookstores, libraries, and even the Internet for more epigrams to add to the pile.

In the process of compiling this book of sailing quotations, I've had to be extremely arbitrary. I started by gathering a selection of quotations and then examined them to see if they could be placed in some sort of categories. As a result, there are sections on sailors, sailing, the sea, and such areas as weather and engines.

Like the sport of sailing, they are sometimes funny and sometimes frightening, but all stand out for an insight into truth or a thoughtful turn of phrase. I could, of course, have filled a book with any of the great sailing writers: Joshua Slocum, Sir Francis Chichester, the Hiscocks, and many others who have encouraged sailors to cast off the docklines for years.

The quotations in this book span the centuries from Homer's *Odyssey* right up to the most recent America's Cup and, as with any collection, there are hundreds more that have been left out either inadvertantly or simply to keep this book manageable. It's up to you, the reader, to add to this collection with your own special quotations, and you'll find blank pages in the back of the book for just that purpose.

Though it was more than 30 years ago, I can still clearly see my father, my mother, and I standing in a boatyard, tired and stained from having just finished painting the bottom of our sailboat. As we watched, a huge sag formed and grew, dragging the thick reddish paint downward into several large drips.

My mother looked at the two of us, shrugged her paint-spattered shoulders, and said cheerfully, "Oh well, you'd never notice it from a galloping horse."

Now, there is a quotation that any sailor can understand.

The Quotable Sailor

On Sailing

Sailing is far more a state of mind and heart than it is a method of getting from Point A to Point B. For many sailors, the simple act of hoisting the sails puts them in a mellow mood, and a destination is far down the list of importance.

This section includes quotations about the art and pleasure of sailing, but it also has reflections on various aspects of sailing that didn't fit elsewhere. Navigation, foreign ports, the mystical art of anchoring—all have been included here because, after all, they are all a part of the sailing experience.

Nothing seems really to matter, that's the charm of it. Whether you get away or whether you don't, whether you arrive at your destination or whether you reach somewhere else, or whether you never get anywhere at all, you're always busy, and you never do anything in particular; and when you're done there's always something else to do, and you can do it if you like, but you'd much better not.

—KENNETH GRAHAME

The best noise in all the world is the rattle of the anchor chain when one comes into harbor at last and lets it go over the bows.

—HILAIRE BELLOC

Here, "the world is too much with us." Out there we are alone. And what a world! A world of water and wind and sky. A world of ever-changing, inexhaustible beauty. A world, moody and capricious, perhaps; but always fair and square. Sometimes soothing and benign, sometimes boisterous and gay, sometimes lowering, threatening, mad, and dangerous; but always giving fair warning, always playing the game with all the cards on the table if we but know them when we see them.

—H. A. CALLAHAN

And I advise all sound cruisers to anchor properly in a harbor, not tie up at a "marina," the yachtsmen's slum.

—SAMUEL ELIOT MORISON

To the visitor whose approach is from the sea, . . . it is first startling, then depressing; but after the island has worked its magic on you, these seedy, shop-soiled towns are accepted. Soon you find yourself regarding them with a rueful affection—like being under the spell of a beautiful woman with flat feet.

—FRANK WIGHTMAN

This is far too much like hard work. The four hours on and four off, the long solitary night watches, the frequent sail changing and reefing down, the incessant motion, all combine to make it quite a strenuous life.

—HUMPHREY BARTON

The way in which land is picked up from the deck or rigging of a small craft is always a fascinating one. The land does not slowly appear out of mist, nor does it come suddenly to stand boldly on the horizon. Rather, it first appears as a vision, as a happy portent arriving out of thin air, out of a vastness of space, to lie with utter humility upon the curved lip of the sea. First, it is not there, then, at the flick of an eyelash, there it is, a flimsy mirage that may or may not be more than a low and wandering cloud.

—RICHARD MAURY

I was at the tiller, when suddenly I shouted: "Look! There's New York!"

Geoff and Nicky bobbed up out of the hatch and vainly searched the skyline ahead.

"I don't see a damned thing except mist," grumbled Geoff.

"I don't mean over there," I replied. "This is our landfall on New York right here!"

They turned and saw I was pointing down into the waters around us. We were sailing through a sea of milk-bottle tops, cardboard cups, orange peel, broken crates and other strange marine life, which told us, as surely as though we had seen the distant towers of Manhattan, that we were drawing near port.

—DENNIS PULESTON

One day, according to my longitude sight, I discovered Idle Hour was inside the walled city of Addis Ababa, capital of Ethiopia!

—Dwight Long

Each noon when we laid down our latitude, Lewis would ask, "How much farther to Brisbane?" And we would carefully measure from the little cross on the chart in miles, then roughly converted the miles into hours, and hours into literature, and answer: "One biography, two detective stories, four *Saturday Evening Posts* and two *Reader's Digests* from Brisbane." Finally when we were only two mystery stories from the continent, we started the motor.

—Ray Kauffman

"Time and chance and Cape Horn: I am still coming at you," I said, and I kept coming until Cape Horn was mine; and for one brief moment in my life, time and chance subdued.

—WEBB CHILES

A knot is never "nearly right"; it is either exactly right or it is hopelessly wrong, one or the other; there is nothing in between.

—CLIFFORD ASHLEY

He picked up the ball of twine and put it to his nose and drew in the smell of boats—caulking smell, rope-locker smell—the smell which, savored in the deepest gloom of wintertime, had the power of evoking faraway sunlit wavetops, a canted mast, splashing bow-waves, a warm summer breeze on a helmsman's cheek.

—JOHN HERSEY

I was completely overwhelmed. I sank down on my knees and thrust my fingers deep into the dry warm sand.

The voyage was over. We were all alive.

—THOR HEYERDAHL

What bliss to be in the cockpit with the sun and the warm breeze on one's skin, just watching the sea, and the sky, and the sails . . .

—SIR FRANCIS CHICHESTER

Overhead, the white sails stretched their arms to catch the night wind. They were my sails—my wings—and they had brought me to the sea of my boyhood dreams.

—WILLIAM ROBINSON

As the years passed, this urge to circle the world alone lay dormant in me, like a gorse seed which will lie in the earth for fifty years until the soil is stirred to admit some air, or light, and the seed suddenly burgeons. And so it was with me.

    —SIR FRANCIS CHICHESTER

How serene to be alone on a well-loved boat on an easy beam reach in smooth water!

    —WILLIAM ROBINSON

The ideal cruise requires a good yacht, pleasant company, and a strange coast with plenty of islands and rocks.

—HUMPHREY BARTON

The fireside is nice and there are those for whom it will be the ultimate Utopia, but the fireside is nicer still when you can remember the joys of an offshore passage and dream of the time when you can go out and do it again.

—TED JONES

I think it is interesting that we have come back to star- and space *ships*. *Jet* will do for a transport shorthand; yet when man really reaches, across the vast seas of space, he still reaches in ships.

—JOHN FOWLES

It takes several years for anyone to learn to handle a yacht reasonably well, and a lifetime to admit how much more there is to learn.

—MAURICE GRIFFITHS

As the miles bubble under the keel, sailors seem to shed skins one after the other until the scales so necessary for living in crowded cities and towns drop away, leaving just the human creature all but naked under the stars. For most, once those scales are gone, they never grow back quite as thick and hard as they once were.

—GEORGE DAY

I stood in the companionway with the warmth from the galley stove against my back and, facing the cold fresh breeze, watched the dark water slowly drown the blinking lights, and Australia was gone.

—RAY KAUFFMAN

What is there about a life afloat that has always appealed to men? It is cold, wet and uncomfortable, often accompanied by bad food and danger.

—T. C. Lethbridge

The lovely thing about cruising is that planning usually turns out to be of little use.

—Dom Degnon

I cannot not sail.

—E. B. White

There is nothing more enticing, disenchanting, and enslaving than the life at sea.

—JOSEPH CONRAD

Cruising is more than a sport. The mood of it comes over you at times, and you can neither work nor rest nor heed another call until you have a deck beneath your feet and point a bowsprit out to sea.

—ARTHUR STURGIS HILDEBRAND

My life has narrowed to a single theme—getting through each day till I round the Horn. The rest of the world has ceased to have any meaning. This is my entire life and there is nothing else.

—NAOMI JAMES

The single commandment of anchoring is "Thou shalt create scope."

—REESE PALLEY

And then again, when you sit at the helm of your little ship on a clear night, and gaze at the countless stars overhead, and realize that you are quite alone on a wide, wide sea, it is apt to occur to you that in the general scheme of things you are merely an insignificant speck on the surface of the ocean; and are not nearly so important nor so self-sufficient as you thought you were. Which is an exceedingly wholesome thought, and one that may effect a permanent change in your deportment that will be greatly appreciated by your friends.

—JAMES S. PITKIN

No aspect of the sailor's world is more mysterious to the landsman than the practice of navigation. To find a precise point in a trackless waste seems neither art nor science, but magic. Yet in no other sphere of progress has the continuity of development been so clearly based on the heritage of the past, nor has the accumulated knowledge been so universally shared by men of all races, creeds and nations.

—CARLETON MITCHELL

We would cut a path just thirteen feet and nine inches across this ocean, like a meteor wandering through the solar system.

—RAY KAUFFMAN

Then we are through. We are inside the harbor. The circle is closed. The dream fulfilled. The vow to myself kept. I have sailed around the world alone.

—WEBB CHILES

Our voyage had commenced, and at last we were away, gliding through the clean water, past the reeds. Care was lifted from our shoulders, for we were free from advice, pessimism, officialism, heat and hot air.

—K. ADLARD COLES

The first feeling the shipwreck gave me was one of incredulity. "It can't happen to me," I muttered as I bit my lip. "Wrecks only happen to other people, because my preparations and my seamanship are too perfect."

—HAL ROTH

When a man weighs anchor in a little ship or a large one he does a jolly thing! He cuts himself off and he starts for freedom and for the chance of things.

—HILAIRE BELLOC

For the first time, and not on paper and in dreams, I had the little ship alone in my hands in a night of velvet dark below and stars above, pushing steadily along into unknown waters. I was extremely happy.

—ARTHUR RANSOME

———

If you haven't run aground, you haven't really been cruising.

—SAILOR'S ADAGE

. . . and the water was as unfathomable as the black holes between the stars at night.

—RAY KAUFFMAN

Again and again that night, I asked myself why I was there—and had no better answer than that perhaps this was the very thing that had drawn me into this voyage: an unexpressed urge to experience a real Cape Horn gale.

—WILLIAM A. ROBINSON

[There is] the deplorable want of taste in our enjoyments which we show by almost totally neglecting the pursuit of what seems to me the highest degree of amusement. This is the sailing ourselves of little vessels of our own, contrived only for our ease and accommodation. This amusement, I confes [sic], if enjoyed in any perfection, would be of the expensive kind: but such expense would not exceed the reach of a moderate fortune and would fall very short of the prices which are daily paid for pleasures of a far inferior rate.

—HENRY FIELDING

The tenuous thread was broken and I was on my own.

—ANN DAVISON

———

Up that rigging, you monkeys. Break out those sails and let them fill with the wind to carry us all to freedom.

—ERROL FLYNN AS CAPT. BLOOD

There is a poetry of sailing as old as the world.

—Antoine de Sainte-Exupery

———

Will anyone dare to tell me that business is more entertaining than fooling around among boats? He must have never seen a boat, or never seen an office, who says so . . .

—Robert Louis Stevenson

The klop, klop of water under the bows of a small boat will cure most troubles in this world, and if another small boat is klop, klopping along within talking distance, and first one and then the other seems to be getting the best out of the wind, worries, however bad, simply disappear.

—ARTHUR RANSOME

To me, nothing made by man is more beautiful than a sailboat under way in fine weather, and to be on that sailboat is to be as close to heaven as I expect to get. It is unalloyed happiness.

—ROBERT MANRY

But now a breeze came up for us astern—a canvas-bellying landbreeze, hale shipmate sent by the singing nymph with sun-bright hair; we made fast the braces, took our thwarts, and let the wind and steersman work the ship with full sail spread all day above our coursing, till the sun dipped, and all the ways grew dark upon the fathomless unresting sea.

—HOMER

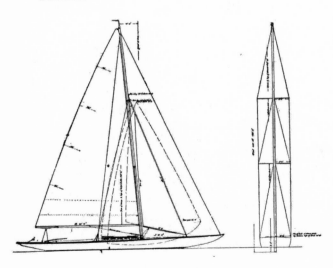

I lay on the bowsprit, facing astern, with the water foaming into spume under me, the masts with every sail white in the moonlight, towering high above me. I became drunk with the beauty and the singing rhythm of it, and for a moment I lost myself—actually lost my life. I was set free! I dissolved in the sea, became white sails and flying spray, became beauty and rhythm, became moonlight and the ship and the high dim-starred sky! I belonged, without past or future, within place and unity and a wild joy, within something greater than my own life, or the life of man, to Life itself. To God, if you want to put it that way.

—EUGENE O'NEILL

I do have this love affair going with the *Lido* . . . It has all the elements of a true love affair: the immunity to outside influences, the times of infatuation, the times of frustration, the reluctance to abuse, the strained patience toward others, the reassurances of a mast hanging along the garage ceiling as snow blows against the doors . . . Sometimes I just stand there in my city clothes at the end of the day for a long time with my hand on the deck. Sometimes, when I do that I can feel the burn of the mainsheet cinched around a wet hand, straining against the wind.

—JOHN JANOVY, JR.

What I know about cruising has been learned almost exclusively from two sources; good books, and a tremendous number of mistakes. Of these two possibilities, I can heartily recommend learning from books, especially if it means avoiding some of the mistakes.

—LOREN R. BORLAND

I can't describe how much I enjoyed that final run for home; the sailing was glorious and I had time to reflect on the race, rescue, Southern Ocean and all that I had experienced. I had seen and learned a lot about myself, both good and bad, and decided I could live with the view.

—PETE GOSS

A sailor's geography is not always that of the cartographer, for whom a cape is a cape, with a latitude and longitude. For the sailor, a great cape is both a very simple and an extremely complicated whole of rocks, currents, breaking seas and huge waves, fair winds and gales, joys and fears, fatigue, dreams, painful hands, empty stomachs, wonderful moments, and suffering at times.

—BERNARD MOITESSIER

Cruising has two main pleasures. One is to go out into wider waters from a sheltered place. The other is to go into a sheltered place from wide waters.

—HOWARD BLOOMFIELD

This is what sailing is about. You sail and sail and sail, enjoying the lovely aspect of God's seas and then you wish for a little change, a bit of adverse weather, something to show off your expertise, perhaps just to prove to yourself you're good at playing the chess game of nature and survival.

—WILLIAM F. BUCKLEY, JR.

Never a ship sails out of the bay, but carries my heart as a stowaway.

—ROSELLE MERCIER MONTGOMERY

The trickiest part of a voyage or cruise may turn out to be the short leg between any harbor entrance and dock, both on the way in and the way out.

—CARLETON MITCHELL

This is one of the very few sports whose techniques never quite match the demands. Throughout a sailing career, we never stop finding new skills to master and new problems to solve.

—JOHN ROUSMANIERE

Sailing does this for me! The world leaps into my eyes and ears, touches me in private places, and afterwards I return to the mainstream of my life renewed.

—HERB PAYSON

I must go down to the sea again, to the lonely sea and the sky. And all I ask is a tall ship and a star to steer her by.

—JOHN MASEFIELD

A cruising life is challenging, interesting, full of variety, sometimes exciting, sometimes frightening, but it's rarely easy.

—LIN AND LARRY PARDEY

There's one thing about bashing to windward. You never forget, for one minute, that you are at sea in a sailing boat.

—TRISTAN JONES

No more expensive way of going really slowly has been invented by man than sailing.

—GARY MULL

Helmsmen will tell you that they keep swinging the boom across the deck of the ship in order to take advantage of the wind, but after weeks of observation it is my opinion that they do it to take advantage of the passengers. The only way to avoid the boom and have any safety at all while sailing is to lie flat on your stomach in the bottom of the ship. This is very uncomfortable on account of the hard boards and because you can't see a thing, but it is the one sure way I know of to go sailing and come back in the boat and not be washed up in the surf.

—James Thurber

The days pass happily with me wherever my ship sails.

—Joshua Slocum

The only record I would cherish would be for the longest circumnavigation, the most dilly-dallying on the way.

—Gwenda Cornell

Nowhere else than upon the sea do the days, weeks and months fall away quicker into the past. They seem to be left astern as easily as the light air-bubbles in the swirls of the ships wake.

—Joseph Conrad

As for myself, the wonderful sea charmed me from the first.

—JOSHUA SLOCUM

Land was created to provide a place for boats to visit.

—BROOKS ATKINSON

You can sail for one day, can't you? That's all it is—one day after another.

—HARRY PIDGEON

The history of seafaring is a part of the study of man, [and] it has its practical side, field work performed in the pleasantest of circumstances, and it is great fun, providing you don't take it too seriously, as if boats were an art form, or human beings, or ideas, or God.

—BASIL GREENHILL

The thrill of sailing and putting out in a boat cannot be expressed in words. It is the feeling of power and the awe of making the wind do your work . . . or putting your strength to the severest test of man and rigging. It is the aesthetic appeal of a beautiful hull and a bleached sail. And it is the quiet noise of water sloshing against the prow as you rest in your berth in the forecastle, absorbing a lifetime of memories.

—ALAN BROWN

Sailing any one of the Seven Seas is a mysterious pleasure, for the fascination and fun of it are so great that they overcome the moments of misfortune and misery we must suffer at sea. We must know heartache to enjoy happiness, and know hunger to enjoy a meal, however good.

—UFFA FOX

"To sail is the thing," wrote Arthur Ransome in his children's classic *Swallows and Amazons*. And just what is that thing? Every sailor knows. It's what the poets say and the pictures show, and everything else, too; it's the joy of casting off and the delight of returning home, and it's all the winds and waves in between. It's the beauty of a boat and the power of the currents, the sound of ratcheting winches and the strain on the wheel; it's the fair breezes and sunsets, the storms and luffing sails. It's the beer in the bar when the race is done, and that moment when you feel you'll never get there. It's what sailors mean when, safe and dry, standing on solid ground, they look at you and say "I'd rather be sailing."

—ANNE DEPUE

If the desire is to sail grandly and the resources are there, it does not do today, any more than during the golden age of the huge J-Boats, to count with progressive dismay the dollars spent.

—WILLIAM F. BUCKLEY, JR.

Even now, with 1,000 little voyages notched in my belt, I still feel a memorial chill on casting off, as the gulls jeer and the empty mainsail claps.

—E. B. WHITE

The thing I realized this last few days is that the earth is a big place.

—PAUL CAYARD

One of the best temporary cures for pride and affectation is seasickness.

—HENRY WHEELER SHOW

Entering port is, I think, the cream of the sport. A strange port, a yacht with no engine, a quiet summer's night and there one has all the makings of a pleasant and most interesting little bit of seamanship.

—HUMPHREY BARTON

The breeze that carries you away from the sweltering city with its din and commotion both cools the brow and clears the mind. No clamoring telephones . . . no appointments to keep, save your anchorage by sundown, and you are on your way with a freshening breeze and lifted sheet.

—W.E. WARRINGTON

A voyage is like a classical drama: it starts slowly and works up with many adventurous incidents to the finish.

—SIR FRANCIS CHICHESTER

To be successful at sea we must keep things simple.

—R.D. (PETE) CULLER

To one given to day dreaming and fond of losing himself in reveries, a sea voyage is full of subjects for meditation: but then they are the wonders of the deep and of the air, and rather tend to abstract the mind from worldly themes. I delighted to loll over the quarter railing or climb to the main top of a calm day, and muse for hours together, on the tranquil bosom of a summer's sea. To gaze upon the piles of golden clouds just peering above the horizon; fancy them some fairy realms and people them with a creation of my own. To watch the gently undulating billows, rolling their silver volumes as if to die away on those happy shores.

—WASHINGTON IRVING

Certainly every man that goes to sea in a little boat of this kind learns terror and salvation, happy living, air, danger, exultation, glory, and repose at the end; and they are not words to him, but, on the contrary, realities which will afterwards throughout his life give the mere words a full meaning.

—HILLAIRE BELLOC

...a single-handed passage in a small sailing boat is about the most expensive way of crossing the Atlantic known to man.

—J.R.L. ANDERSON

One thing had impressed us deeply on this little voyage: the great world dropped away very quickly . . . The matters of great importance we had left were not important . . . We had lost the virus, or it had been eaten by the anti-bodies of quiet. Our pace had slowed greatly; the hundred thousand small reactions of our daily world were reduced to very few.

—JOHN STEINBECK

What is more pleasant than a friendly little yacht, a long stretch of smooth water, a gentle breeze, the stars?

—WILLIAM ATKIN

The best blood-sports are those where the only life in jeopardy is the sportsman's. Rock-climbing is one of these—but perhaps too lethal an example, since real addicts do not commonly live beyond middle age. Single-handed cruising is another.

—FRANCOISE LEGRANDE

On the Sea

For centuries, man has gazed at the sea in awe and fear. For centuries, it served as a frontier beyond which no one would venture and, even after man learned to navigate the oceans, they remain an untamed challenge to men and their ships.

Like their boats, man has attributed human characteristics to the sea, calling it beautiful as well as menacing. Sailors love the sea much of the time, hate it some of the time, and the wise ones have a healthy fear of it all the time.

For all at last return to the sea—to Oceanus, the ocean river, like the everflowing river of time, the beginning and the end.

—RACHEL CARSON

Waves are not measured in feet or inches, they are measured in increments of fear.

—BUZZY TRENT

I wanted freedom, open air, adventure. I found it on the sea.

—ALAIN GERBAULT

The ocean has always been a salve to my soul . . . the best thing for a cut or abrasion was to go swimming in salt water. Later down the road of life, I made the discovery that salt water was also good for the mental abrasions one inevitably acquires on land.

—JIMMY BUFFETT

The sea drives truth into a man like salt.

—HILAIRE BELLOC

The sea never changes and its works, for all the talk of men, are wrapped in mystery.

—JOSEPH CONRAD

The cure for anything is salt water—sweat, tears, or the sea.

—ISAK DINESEN

Neither nature nor art has partitioned the sea into empires. The ocean and its treasures are the common property of all men.

—JOHN ADAMS

———•••—

I have known the sea too long to believe in its respect for decency.

—JOSEPH CONRAD

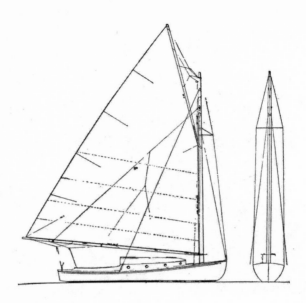

The sea is at its best at London, near midnight, when you are within the arms of a capacious chair, before a glowing fire, selecting phases of the voyages you will never make.

—H. M. TOMLINSON

The sea hates a coward.

—Eugene O'Neill

The ocean is an object of no small terror.

—Edmund Burke

Most of us, I suppose, are a little nervous of the sea. No matter what its smiles may be, we doubt its friendship.

—H. M. Tomlinson

Love of the sea is a strange, unaccountable emotion.
—CHARLES VIOLET

They that go down to the sea in ships,
that do business in great waters;
These see the works of the Lord,
and his wonders in the deep.
—PSALM 107

The sea finds out everything you did wrong.

—Francis Stokes

He who lets the sea lull him into a false sense of security is in very grave danger.

—Hammond Innes

I wanted only two things: to feel well again, and to be back on terra firma. Neither seemed likely.

—Tom Wicker

It's out there at sea that you are really yourself.
—Vito Dumas

———•••———

The sea belongs to us all, and every aspect of it, from halcyon calm to howling hurricane, is fraught with beauty.
—Samuel Eliot Morison

Whenever your preparations for sea are poor, the sea worms its way in and finds the problems.

—FRANCIS STOKES

I was born in the breezes, and I had studied the sea as perhaps few men have studied it, neglecting all else.

—JOSHUA SLOCUM

Dawn at sea breaks high in the sky: a faint flush on the highest peaks of the clouds. Then the miracle starts that never fails to make man humble: the momentous occurrence of the earth's creation. One moment, darkness is upon the face of the deep and the spirit of God moves upon the waters; the next moment, there is light. The young sailor will see the light and feel, more than he understands, why God called the light Day and the darkness Night, and rested.

—JAN DE HARTOG

The clearest night skies I have ever seen anywhere were over the lake. Out in the ocean, well clear of the land, perhaps a thousand miles out, the skies are crammed with stars, but on Titicaca there was hardly room for the black sky among the stars! The bright planets and all the major stars were like small moons, their rotundity clearly delineated. The man-made satellites were immediately obvious, like taxi-cabs on the Epsom Downs course on Derby Day. There were literally a million bodies in the sky.

—TRISTAN JONES

Perhaps in some future age, when sails and their use are as forgotten as the ox cart, humans will roam the floor of the sea. Only then will man's conquest of his planet be complete. Thus, the ocean is the ultimate challenge, as it was the first.

—CARLETON MITCHELL

Unfathomable Sea! whose waves are years!
Ocean of time, whose waters of deep woe
Are brackish with the salt of human tears!
Thou shoreless flood which in thy ebb and flow
Claspest the limits of mortality . . .

—PERCY BYSSHE SHELLEY

Flatter not yourself that good luck is judgment and discretion, for all your eggs could have foundered if the spirit of the sea had just said the word.

—HERMAN MELVILLE

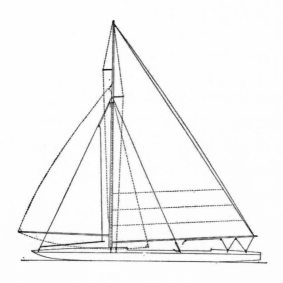

In the artificial world of his cities and towns, man often forgets the true nature of his planet. The sense of all these things comes to him most clearly in the course of a long ocean voyage, when he watches day after day the receding rim of the horizon, ridged and furrowed by waves . . . And then, as never on land, he knows the truth that his world is a water world, a planet dominated by its covering mantle of ocean, in which the continents are but transient intrusions of land above the all-encircling sea.

—RACHEL CARSON

The sea had its drawbacks, though: there was no doubt about that. It couldn't give you a formal education (or even a well-balanced informal one), or love or a helping hand when you needed it. The sea was cold, disinterested, impartial. There was no real warmth to it, no sharing of knowledge or feelings. And yet there was one hugely wonderful thing to be said for the sea: it was always the sea. It was the sea and nothing else. It couldn't dissimulate. It couldn't say one thing while thinking another. It couldn't flatter you and turn your head. There wasn't a treacherous or dishonest wave in its whole massive body.

—ROBERT MANRY

The sea—this truth must be confessed—has no generosity. No display of manly qualities—courage, hardihood, endurance, faithfulness—has ever been known to touch its irresponsible consciousness of power. The ocean has the conscienceless temper of a savage autocrat spoiled by much adulation. The sea cannot brook the slightest appearance of defiance, and has remained the irreconcilable enemy of ships and men ever since ships and men had the unheard-of audacity to go afloat together in the face of its frown.

—JOSEPH CONRAD

A great cape, for us, can't be expressed in longitude and latitude alone. A great cape has a soul, with very soft, very violent shadows and colors. A soul as smooth as a child's, as hard as a criminal's. And that is why we go.

—Bernard Moitessier

The sea has many voices. Listen to the surf, really lend it your ears, and you will hear in it a world of sounds: hollow boomings and heavy roarings, great watery tumblings and tramplings, long hissing seethes, sharp, rifle-shot reports, splashes, whispers, the grinding undertone of stones, and sometimes vocal sounds that might be the half-heard talk of people in the sea.

—Henry Beston

In certain places, at certain hours, gazing at the sea is dangerous. It is what looking at a woman sometimes is.

—VICTOR HUGO

Like a savage tigress that tossing in the jungle overlays her own cubs, so the sea smashes even the mightiest whales against the rocks, and leaves them there side by side with the split wrecks of ships. No mercy, no power but its own controls it. Panting and snorting like a mad battle steed that has lost its rider, the masterless ocean overruns the globe.

—HERMAN MELVILLE

O'er the glad waters
of the dark blue sea,
our thoughts as boundless,
and our souls as free.

      —LORD BYRON

Not only is the sea unspoiled and without artificiality, there is a primeval quality, a purity surrounding its environment. Maybe you appreciate the sea because when you are lost upon its vastness your life is not jammed up with the trivia, the meaningless detail, and the foolish stuff of civilization.

      —HAL ROTH

The elation that is felt at speed, running before the wind and sea, may be so great as to overcome the seamanlike caution the ocean demands, but sooner or later the sea will catch up with you.

—HAL ROTH

A man who is not afraid of the sea will soon be drowned, he said, for he will be going out on a day he shouldn't. But we do be afraid of the sea, and we do only be drownded [sic] now and again.

—JOHN SYNGE

But you must at all times remember that the power of the sea is greater than anything else on earth; and that although many fleets have sailed over it, not one has conquered or harnessed it, and no one ever will. Remember too, that like fire, the sea is a good friend but a bad master, so you must never, never allow yourself to get into a position where the sea takes control.

—UFFA FOX

You can out-think the ocean, but you can't out-slug the ocean.

—SIGN AT U.S. NAVAL ACADEMY

I really don't know why it is that all of us are so committed to the sea, except I think it's because in addition to the fact that the sea changes, and the light changes, and ships change, it's because we all came from the sea. All of us have in our veins the exact same percentage of salt in our blood that exists in the ocean, and therefore we have salt in our blood, in our sweat, in our tears. We are tied to the ocean. And when we go back to the sea—whether it is to sail or to watch it—we are going back from whence we came.

—JOHN F. KENNEDY, AMERICA'S CUP '62

If you would know the age of the earth, look upon the sea in a storm. The greyness of the whole immense surface, the wind furrows upon the faces of the waves, the great masses of foam, tossed about and waving, like matted white locks, give to the sea in a gale an appearance of hoary age, lustreless, dull, without gleams, as though it had been created before light itself.

—JOSEPH CONRAD

I am an optimist about things in general, but I look upon the sea as the ancients view their gods, with superstition.

—E.A. PYE

The sea belongs to us all, and every aspect of it, from halcyon calm to howling hurricane, is fraught with beauty.
—Samuel Eliot Morison

The sea continues to feed our spiritual need for adventure into the unknown.
—Robert Ballard

When I forget how talented God is, I look to the sea.
—WHOOPI GOLDBERG

On looking to windward, he beheld the green masses of water that were rolling in towards the land, with a violence that seemed irresistible, crowned with ridges of foam; and there were moments when the air appeared filled with sparkling gems, as the rays of the rising sun fell upon the spray that was swept from wave to wave.
—JAMES FENIMORE COOPER

The sea evokes in me infinite thoughts and moods; serenity, turmoil, the beginning of life, the unconquerable end. Majestic, awesome, often cruel but always indescribably beautiful.

—RICARDO MONTALBAN

The sea provides visions, darknesses, revelations.

—HILAIRE BELLOC

In the sea, I realize the hidden purposes of all things.

—LIV ULLMANN

We were once more upon the ocean, where sky and water meet.

—RICHARD HENRY DANA

When I look to the sea I see peaceful and powerful infinity.

—LOU GOSSETT, JR.

The sea lures the unwary with the promise of freedom, but it harbors great risk.

—HAYDEN STONE

On Sailors

This is a section about sailors, about us—you and me—and those who populate our nautical world.

I think you will find, as I did, that these quotations will strike a chord within you. Surely you will recognize yourself here, and perhaps you will be reminded of crew, shipmates, or just passing acquaintances in the thoughts found here.

Happy Adventure puttered blindly on into the dark and brooding murk and I was soon fog-chilled, unutterably lonely, and scared to death. Since rum is a known and accepted antidote for all three conditions I took a long, curative drink for each separate ailment.

—FARLEY MOWAT

I started celebrating my birthday drinking a bottle of wine . . . sitting in the cockpit with a champagne cocktail . . . full rig, smoking jacket, smart new trousers, black shoes, etc. The only slipup is that I have left my bow-tie behind, and have had to use an ordinary black tie.

—SIR FRANCIS CHICHESTER

I decided that keeping watch was a waste of time, went below and mixed myself my anti-scorbutic. The lemon juice . . . not only keeps physical scurvy away, but if enough of the right kind of whisky is added to it, mental scurvy as well. *Gipsy Moth* sailed on through the dark.

—SIR FRANCIS CHICHESTER

The sound of the chain dragging along the bottom brought me to my senses quicker than a bucket of cold water.

—E. A. PYE

I imagined that others, too, would be impelled to throw over the routine that stifles life and open their minds.

—Vito Dumas

A day or so before reaching port there would be a great primping and grooming of shore clothes and the body lavished with attention. A very few minutes after the vessel was secured to the wharf an assembly of total strangers appeared momentarily on deck and then disappeared in the direction of the local settlement as fast as they could go.

—Ernest K. Gann

Men need harbors almost as much as they need the gods.

—Hilaire Belloc

A tourist remains an outsider throughout his visit, but a sailor is part of the local scene from the moment he arrives.

—Ann Davison

We had twelve hours of daylight, and if we did not sight the coast, I should conclude that Brazil was merely a geographical expression.

—FRANK WIGHTMAN

I became really worried when my dead-reckoning put me on top of a hill a hundred feet high, and there was no land in sight!

—E. A. PYE

Of all irritating things that can happen on board ship nothing surpasses the splash of large raindrops on your face when you are immersed in the early hours of sleep. At first you pretend to yourself that you have dreamed about them; you draw the blanket over your head, and recommence sleeping with iron determination. They become more and more insistent. You curse quietly and bitterly for a moment, then you leap up, tossing off your blanket. A frenzied argument follows with the approaching squall. Blankets and pillows are hurled below and after a few parting oaths you retire to sulk on the uncomfortable mess in your bunk.

—EDWARD H. DODD, JR.

We have so far remained reasonably civilized but I for one am slowly but inevitably deteriorating over small matters. I used, for instance, to fold up neatly my sleeping bag and eiderdown and stow them properly in the recess at the end of my bunk. Now I just kick them all in higgledy-piggledy down into the recess, pushing them well home with my feet, throw in a garment or two after them, stuff in my bolster (half the International Code of Flags), bung up the entrance to the cavern with my pillow. I even use my egg spoon to stir my tea with now.

—HUMPHREY BARTON

There was no sextant aboard. I had priced one at Tenerife and the cost appalled me. It seemed better to buy four pounds' worth of provisions and take a slightly longer time to make the journey. I had no intention of paying forty-five pounds for a sextant and its related tables for the sake of saving a mere seven or eight days. After all, if Columbus could cross the Atlantic without a chart, it seemed reasonable that I could do it without a sextant. If I did not hit Canada, I'd run ashore at Argentina—or somewhere in between.

—Francis Brenton

The five of us divided the watches, moving in progression in a system so complicated that an argument invariably arose every four hours.

—EDWARD H. DODD, JR.

The San Francisco waterfront abounds in salty characters, many of whom have an easy command of nautical terminology, a vast knowledge of all that pertains to ships and the sea, and practically no experience beyond the end of the dock.

—ERNEST K. GANN

We picture the sailor's life in terms of adventure and romance. We think of the sailor as someone who has seen life widely; but in point of fact there is no class of person who is less familiar with what is held ordinarily to constitute life. In consequence, he retains that freshness, almost amounting to an innocence of outlook, that is his particular and peculiar charm.

—ALEC WAUGH

Men in a ship are always looking up, and men ashore generally looking down.

—JOHN MASEFIELD

To young men contemplating a voyage I would say go.

—Joshua Slocum

At sea, I learned how little a person needs, not how much.

—Robin Lee Graham

Asked how he slept after losing the first race of the 1974 America's Cup, Sir James Hardy replied, "Like a baby. Woke up every two hours and cried."

He set a regal cap on his famous victory, in the true style of the outrageous character we all know him to be. In the middle of the post-match press conference, he collapsed, heroically drunk, with an empty bottle of rum still gripped in his fist.

It was a display of gloriously drunken joy. And, of course, it was frowned upon by the committee of the New York Yacht Club. Rather than frowning, they should have installed a brass commemorative plaque in the place where Turner fell, for this was without doubt the last great gesture of carefree amateur recklessness that would ever be seen in the America's Cup.

—JOHN BERTRAND, DESCRIBING TED TURNER AFTER WINNING THE AMERICA'S CUP

He who goes to sea for pleasure would go to Hell for a pastime.

—SAMUEL JOHNSON

Of course I am lonely at sea, but one suffers less on the ocean in that respect than in the heart of London.

—SIR WALTER RALEIGH

Only fools and passengers drink at sea.

—ALAN VILLIERS

A sailor is an artist whose medium is the wind.
—WEBB CHILES

Sailors, with their built-in sense of order, service, and discipline, should really be running the world.
—NICHOLAS MONSARRAT

A sailor's wonderfully handy about the house.
—DOROTHY SAYERS

Life is too short to splice wire rope.

—Bernard Moitessier

———•••••———

Only two sailors, in my experience, never ran aground. One never left port and the other was an atrocious liar.

—Don Bamford

Out of sight of land the sailor feels safe. It is the beach that worries him.

—CHARLES G. DAVIS

No amount of skill, no equipment, and no boat will keep you from disaster if you don't develop the most important seagoing skill of all, a complete fear of falling overboard.

—LIN AND LARRY PARDEY

To be truly challenging, a voyage, like a life, must rest on a firm foundation of financial unrest. Otherwise you are doomed to a routine traverse, the kind known to yachtsmen, who play with their boats at sea—"cruising," it is called. Voyaging belongs to seamen, and to the wanderers of the world who cannot, or will not, fit in.

—STERLING HAYDEN

No man will be a sailor who has contrivance enough to get himself into a jail; for being in a ship is being in a jail, with the chance of being drowned. A man in jail has more room, better food, and commonly better company.

—SAMUEL JOHNSON

Sailors have made a good bargain with the world. We get to borrow it, play with it and be released from its deadening grip. We get to use it without owning it.

—REESE PALLEY

Cruising sailors make lists like stagnant water makes mosquitoes.
—REESE PALLEY

The three major factors to consider in a successful crewman are attitude, attitude, and attitude.
—DENNIS CONNER

The only way to get a good crew is to marry one.
—ERIC HISCOCK

A sailing ship is no democracy; you don't caucus a crew as to where you'll go any more than you inquire when they'd like to shorten sail.

—STERLING HAYDEN

I know who you are, but you'll have to wipe your feet.

—CAPT. RICHARD BROWN OF THE SCHOONER *AMERICA* TO PRINCE ALBERT OF ENGLAND, 1851

No one is lonelier than a sailing ship captain.

—ALAN VILLIERS

Hereafter, if you should observe an occasion to give your officers and friends a little more praise than is their due, and confess more fault than you can justly be charged with, you will only become the sooner for it, a great captain.

—BENJAMIN FRANKLIN TO JOHN PAUL JONES, 1780

Familiarity with danger makes a brave man braver, but less daring. Thus with seamen: he who goes the oftenest round Cape Horn goes the most circumspectly.

—HERMAN MELVILLE

My idea of getting off in a boat is to get as far away from telephones as possible.

—RODERICK STEPHENS

It's a good thing the old man died before yachts made of veneering and manned with gigolo yacht jockies appeared.

—L. FRANCIS HERRESHOFF ABOUT HIS FATHER,
NATHANAEL G. HERRESHOFF

It seems odd that it should take about three weeks of a voyage before one can begin to enjoy it, but so it is, or seemed so then to me.

—Sir Francis Chichester

"I am the Captain of the Pinafore
And a right good captain too!
And I'm never ever sick at sea!"
"What, never?"
"No, never!"
"What, never?"
"Hardly ever!"
"He's hardly ever sick at sea!
Then give three cheers and one cheer more,
For the hardy Captain of the *Pinafore*!"

—Gilbert & Sullivan

The art of the sailor is to leave nothing to chance.

—ANNIE VAN DE WIELE

———————

Any damn fool can circumnavigate the world sober.
It takes a really good sailor to do it drunk.

—SIR FRANCIS CHICHESTER, LOADING HIS BOAT WITH GIN

———————

It isn't that life ashore is distasteful to me. But life at
sea is better.

—SIR FRANCIS DRAKE

I must confess that many times, when I saw my sails in ribbons and my poor boat struggling desperately on a raging sea, plunging down terrific precipices, disappearing under monstrous waves that threaten to swallow her, then pointing her bows to the black skies as if to implore the mercy of Him whose will disposes of life and death, yes, many times I said to myself: "If I get away with it this time, I'll never set foot on a boat again."

—MARCEL BARDINAUX

Adventure means risking something. And it is when we are doing that, that we know what a splendid thing life is and how splendidly it can be lived. The man who never dares never does. The man who never risks never wins. It is far better to venture and fail than to lie on the hearth rug like a sleepily purring cat. Only fools laugh at failure. Wise men laugh at the lazy and the too contented, and at those who are so timid that they dare undertake nothing.

—ALAIN GERBAULT

If you sawed open that boy's head, there'd be a boat in there.

—CAPT. ROY CAMPBELL, DESCRIBING ANOTHER SKIPPER

Whenever I find myself growing grim about the mouth; whenever it is a damp drizzly November in my soul; whenever I find myself involuntarily pausing before coffin warehouses, and bringing up the rear of every funeral I meet; and especially whenever my hypos get such an upper hand of me, that it requires a strong moral principle to prevent me from deliberately stepping into the street, and methodically knocking people's hats off—then, I account it high time to get to sea as soon as I can.

—HERMAN MELVILLE

Was there ever a sailor free to choose that didn't settle somewhere near the sea?

—RUDYARD KIPLING

Any fool can carry on, but a wise man knows how to shorten sail in time.

—JOSEPH CONRAD

No one but an acrobat or a sailor could have got up to that bell-rope from the bracket, and no one but a sailor could have made the knots with which the cord was fastened to the chair.

—SHERLOCK HOLMES (SIR ARTHUR CONAN DOYLE)

The wonder is always new that any sane man can be a sailor.

—RALPH WALDO EMERSON

I never knew a sailor, in my life, who would not prefer a pot of hot coffee or chocolate, on a cold night, to all the rum afloat.

—RICHARD HENRY DANA

A sailor's joys are as simple as a child's.

—BERNARD MOITESSIER

Upon acquiring his first boat, the yachtsman discovers that its use is going to involve intimate personal contact with rope and cordage, and to a far greater extent than he ever anticipated.

—HERVEY GARRETT SMITH

When a man comes to like a sea life, he is not fit to live on land.

—DR. SAMUEL JOHNSON

To be locked up in a small, unprivate, jostling space capsule with strange people for several weeks is like being placed in a culture breeding flask in a laboratory. Any small infection is bound to wax, swell, and break out in epidemic proportions. The ideal crewmember is a rare creature indeed. He has the coolness, courage and derring-do of James Bond; the inventiveness and mechanical skills of Tom Swift; the agility and strength of an Olympic decathlon winner; and the winning ways and affableness of a graduate summa cum laude of the Dale Carnegie Institute of charm.

—WILLIAM SNAITH

I'll take a crew of experienced sailors. Each of them will know intuitively where all the gear is stowed. He knows the perils of eating or drinking too much. Or too little. He can steer, pilot, handle sail and navigate. He never drops shaving brushes into the toilet bowl. He has single-handed on occasion. He is neat and seamanlike. Silent without being morose. Doesn't whistle. Knows how tired I am and stands my watches without complaint. Naturally, my ideal crew would consist entirely of skippers.

—ALFRED E. LOOMIS

To the question, "When were your spirits at their lowest ebb?" the obvious answer seemed to be, "When the gin gave out".

—Sir Francis Chichester

We study the sailor, the man of his hands, man of all work; all eye, all finger, muscle, skill & endurance; a tailor, a carpenter, cooper, stevedore, & clerk & astronomer besides. He is a great saver, and a great quiddle by the necessity of his situation.

—Ralph Waldo Emerson

With so many sharp bones protruding, I was covered in a multitude of bruises, which ranged through every colour from dirty orange to bright purple. On favourite spots like my knees and thighs they were arranged in clusters like exhibits at the Chelsea Flower Show. I was well practised in moving around the boat carefully, but when every single object was sharp, jutting or just plain hard, it was impossible to escape them all the time. It was a matter of clinging on and dodging the bits of boat as they came at you.

—CLARE FRANCIS

Of all those I have met with who have travelled on land or sea alone, not one has told me it was "lonely".

—JOHN MACGREGOR

I have noticed that most men, when they enter a barber shop and must wait their turn, drop into a chair and pick up a magazine. I simply sit down and pick up the thread of my sea wandering, which began more than fifty years ago and is not quite ended. There is hardly a waiting room in the east that has not served as my cockpit, whether I was waiting to board a train or to see a dentist. And I am usually still trimming sheets when the train starts or the drill begins to whine.

—E.B. WHITE

I never found naval men at a loss. Tell them to do anything that is not impossible and depend upon it, they will do it.

—DUKE OF WELLINGTON

Landfall and Departure mark the rhythmical swing of a seaman's life.

—JOSEPH CONRAD

In no other trade or calling can you discover such men who have been tempered and formed by their daily environment, the sea

—DOUGLAS REEMAN

Bad cooking is responsible for more trouble at sea than all other things put together.

—THOMAS FLEMING DAY

On Boats

Because a sailor's life literally depends on his boat, it's no surprise that boats often take on larger-than-life and almost mystical personalities. We tend to credit our boats with a thought process and even human characteristics, such as being sweet, recalcitrant, or ill-tempered.

Sailors always refer to their boats as "she" and, in this politically correct world, that can often be misunderstood by those whose feet are firmly planted on shore. The fact of the matter is that the gender isn't intended as a slight but rather as a tribute to the great faith and love that we invest in our boats.

Believe me, my young friend, there is nothing—absolutely nothing—half so much worth doing as simply messing about in boats.

—KENNETH GRAHAME

Of all the living creatures upon the land and sea, it is ships alone that cannot be taken in by barren pretenses, that will not put up with bad art from their masters.

—JOSEPH CONRAD

The cabin of a small yacht is truly a wonderful thing; not only will it shelter you from the tempest, but from the other troubles of life; it is a safe retreat.

  —L. FRANCIS HERRESHOFF

I suppose I must be one of the few men alive who can remember what life was like in the American Navy of sailing ships. All those fine old ships have sailed away into the Land of Dreams, mounting the swell like great birds. No smoke, no vibration, no noise except the occasional slatting of a reef point against the sail.

  —REAR ADM. DANIEL MANNIX III

There is no call to go talking of pushing and pulling. Boats are quite tricky enough for those that sit still without looking further for the cause of trouble.

—J.R.R. TOLKIEN

If you can't repair it, maybe it shouldn't be on board.

—LIN AND LARRY PARDEY

I don't own a boat. But I have a lot of friends with boats, which anyone can tell you is a lot better.

—ROBERT STONE

Ships are the nearest things to dreams that hands have ever made.

—Robert N. Rose

Ⅰ have built barns and houses and I know the peculiar trait such things have of running past their estimated cost. This knowledge was mine, was already mine, when I estimated the probable cost of the building of the *Snark* at $7,000. Well, she cost $30,000. Now, don't ask me, please. It is the truth. I signed the checks and raised the money. Of course, there is no explaining it.

—Jack London

There is something about boats which makes one feel they are living creatures—each as different from her sisters as human beings are from each other. The very fact that that one refers to a boat as "she" shows that since time began men have loved their boats.

—FRANCIS KINNEY

Of all man-made things there is nothing so lovely as a sailboat. It is a living thing with a soul and feelings—responsive as a saddle horse, loyal as a dog, and thoroughly downright decent. Every sailboat has a character all its own. No builder has ever succeeded in turning out two boats exactly alike. Their measurements may be identical, but the difference is in their character.

—H. A. CALLAHAN

Anything that rots, gets itself eaten by various critters of the sea, and soaks up water cannot be the ultimate boat-building material. And no material that smells like a burned toothbrush, sweats like a beer bottle and was developed entirely for the sake of production-line efficiency could be expected to be entirely wonderful, either . . .

There is just no such thing as a perfect boat building material. All have serious faults, severe limitations and desirable qualities . . .

And each can produce a boat that if properly designed, built, used and maintained, will last far longer than you and I. The sadness is that too few, far too few, boats get their fair share of those four things.

—BILL ROTHROCK

When morning came we were plunging through the sunlit sea under winged-out fore and main, the *Dolphin* careering along joyously like a hobbyhorse on the dewy green of an unmowed lawn.

—DESMOND HOLDRIDGE

There is little man has made that approaches anything in nature, but a sailing ship does. There is not much man has made that calls to all the best in him, but a sailing ship does.

—ALAN VILLIERS

But nobody has found a substitute for the sweet chuckling of water like the laughter of young girls, that you hear outside the hull while lying in a small yacht's bunk.

—SAMUEL ELIOT MORISON

Most everyone who has inherited a love of the sea feels that the clipper bow is a befitting finial to a sailing vessel, as a beautiful head of hair is to a woman. Perhaps neither the long hair nor the bowsprit is necessary, but when either is removed there is a loss of character that is hard to replace.

—L. FRANCIS HERRESHOFF

Possibly this love for a small cabin was atavistic, derived from our remote ancestors for whom a cave was the only safe, indeed the only possible dwelling.

—SAMUEL ELIOT MORISON

The perfection of a yacht's beauty is that nothing should be there for only beauty's sake.

—JOHN MACGREGOR

I hated to go ashore, for the boat looked smaller every time I left. Then one fine morning I awoke, looked more closely at my floating home, and saw everything in its true perspective: the *Nengo* wasn't small, she was compact.

—Francis Brenton

The desire to build a house is the tired wish of a man content thenceforward with a single anchorage. The desire to build a boat is the desire of youth, unwilling yet to accept the idea of a final resting place.

—Arthur Ransome

A comfortable boat, it now seemed to me, was one which, in offshore cruising, would round a headland with a certain amount of discomfort and be snug in harbor while the beamy family boat was still slogging into it.

—ALFRED LOOMIS

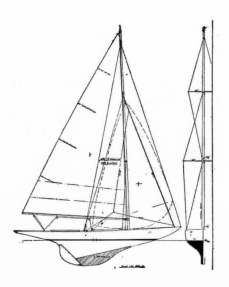

But, indeed, nowadays, what with their boats made like spoons and their boats made like tableknives, and their boats made like tops, and their boats made like scoopers, and their boats made like half-boats, cut away in the middle, no one can tell whether a boat is Choctaw, Eskimo, or Papuan. For boats have nowadays fallen into chaos, like everything else.

—Hilaire Belloc

I no longer had the sensation of traveling but a feeling of living an isolated life on an island forty-five feet long.

—Ray Kauffman

The greatest difference between the beautiful yacht and the plain one is the way their crews treat them, for the crew of the beautiful yacht usually gives her tender loving care. They realize that all of their work will show to advantage, while the crew of the plain yacht has learned from experience that nothing they can do will help much, for the sailorman at heart is still a romanticist.

—L. FRANCIS HERRESHOFF

There are only two colors to paint a boat, black or white, and only a fool would paint a boat black.

—NATHANAEL G. HERRESHOFF

For one thing, I was no longer alone; a man is never alone with the wind—and the boat made three.

—Hilaire Belloc

I wriggled into my sleeping-bag and gave the wood by my ear an approving pat. Damning all hotel rooms, I went to sleep.

—Charles Landery

That is why I got a small boat of my own, so that I can poke along at my leisure, visiting remote corners of the earth and actually seeing how the other half of the world lives.

—DWIGHT LONG

It is impossible, in this world, to achieve an idea; and if you do not believe this, I recommend you to take a picture of your perfect ship out of your mind's eye and try to copy it exactly in metal and canvas and wood.

—WESTON MARTYR

If you cannot arrive in daylight, then stand off well clear, all night, and wait until dawn. After all, that's one of the things God made boats for—to wait in.
　　　　—TRISTAN JONES

There is but a plank between a sailor and eternity.
　　　　—THOMAS GIBBONS

A small craft in the ocean is, or should be, a benevolent dictatorship.
　　　　—TRISTAN JONES

You have no right to own a yacht if you ask that question.

—J. P. MORGAN, SR., IN ANSWER TO A QUESTION BY HENRY CLAY PIERCE OF HOW MUCH IT COSTS TO OWN AND RUN A YACHT

If a man must be obsessed by something, I suppose a boat is as good as anything, perhaps a bit better than most.

—E. B. WHITE

What a joy is a sweet-smelling, spotless cabin, with all clothes neatly stowed high and dry. What a joy to sit in such a cabin under the soft glow of a kerosene lamp and study the chart for an even more snug and romantic cove than the one you are anchored in and lay a course to regions even farther from the maddening crowds: places where men are sailors or farmers and can converse directly with the gods and can feel the pulse of nature . . .

—L. FRANCIS HERRESHOFF

I received in succession our stores, and stored the cargo as best I could while the dinghy sank lower and lower in the water, and its precarious super-structure grew higher.

—ERSKINE CHILDERS

If H-28's design is only slightly changed, the whole balance may be thrown out. If you equip her with deadeyes, build her with sawn frames, or fill her virgin bilge with ballast, the birds will no longer carol over her, nor will the odors arising from the cabin make poetry, nor will your soul be fortified against a world of warlords, politicians and fakers.

—L. FRANCIS HERRESHOFF

Up aloft you hang on. Beyond the breakwater the wild Atlantic growls. Plumes of spray pounce on lighthouse windows . . . Up here, you feel the motion more. You feel her reach out over a sea and hang; then down she goes with a sickening rush, and the second after the crash your mast goes buckling forward with a sideways motion. You wonder how wood can take it.

—STERLING HAYDEN

I want a boat that drinks six, eats four, and sleeps two.

—ERNEST K. GANN

I

The cruiser, the strong little, deep little boat . . . is a complete satisfaction for man.

—HILAIRE BELLOC

I

In little vessels, there is joy. In large vessels there is travail and perplexity.

—ERNEST K. GANN

. . . over the breaking billows, with bellying sail,
And foaming beak, like a flying bird . . .
> —*BEOWULF*

A ship is always referred to as "she" because it costs
so much to keep her in paint and powder.
> —ADM. CHESTER NIMITZ

It looks like frozen snot.
> —L. FRANCIS HERRESHOFF, LOOKING AT A HERRESHOFF
> BULLSEYE BUILT OF FIBERGLASS

The ship, a fragment detached from the earth, went on lonely and swift like a small planet.

—JOSEPH CONRAD

Yacht design, as carried on at present, is rather like making love to a woman. The approach is completely empirical. At the end, the male, even though he might be successful, usually had no idea of just how and why he had succeeded.

—PROF. E. J. RICHARDS

The craft pranced and reared, and plunged like an animal. As each wave came, and she rose for it, she seemed like a horse making at a fence outrageously high. The manner of her scramble over these walls of water is a mystic thing, and, moreover, at the top of them were ordinarily these problems in white water, the foam racing down from the summit of each wave, requiring a new leap, and a leap from the air. Then, after scornfully bumping a crest, she would slide, and race, and splash down a long incline and arrive bobbing and nodding in front of the next menace.

—STEPHEN CRANE

I have another theory, one which I think can be proved, that good-looking boats last longer than plain ones. The boat that gives one pleasure merely to look at it is a great joy, evoking favorable comment from others. This fills the owner with pride, causing him to take extra care with the boat's appearance.

—JOEL WHITE

A small sailing craft is not only beautiful, it is seductive and full of strange promise and the hint of trouble. If it happens to be an auxiliary cruising boat, it is without question the most compact and ingenious arrangement for living ever devised by the restless mind of man.

—E. B. WHITE

Any boat that can outsail your own boat is (a) crewed by professionals, (b) dangerously light and underbuilt, or (c) a hot high-tech expensive racing boat.

—CHUCK GUSTAFSON

Ⓢ

The number of people that a sailboat can comfortably daysail is equal to the number of berths claimed by the builder. The number of people that a sailboat can comfortably sleep is the number of berths claimed by the builder divided by three.

—CHUCK GUSTAFSON

In the Great Age of Velcro, rope, knots, and all things done with them seem charmingly irrelevant. Then you step aboard a sailboat and realize that the rules have changed.

—David Seidman

Just as beauty in woman creates allure and inspires affection, so it does in a boat.

—William Snaith

Knowing your vessel is everything; each one is a law unto herself. Some pretty fancy maneuvering can be done by a skipper who has learned his ship's idiosyncrasies.

—Donald Hamilton

"Do you know, I've never been in a boat in all my life?""What?" cried the Rat, openmouthed: "Never been in a—you never—well, I—what have you been doing, then?"

—KENNETH GRAHAME

When, staunchly entering port, after long ventures, hauling up, worn and old, batter'd by sea and wind, torn by many a fight, with the original sails all gone, replaced or mended, I only saw, at last, the beauty of the ship . . .

—WALT WHITMAN

Boats, like whiskey, are all good.

—R.D. (PETE) CULLER

The cardinal rule of good taste in all design, on land or sea, is honesty of purpose.

—John G. Hanna

Each boat seems to contain a personality which manifests itself in the way she takes a sea.

—William Snaith

A lot of sentimental rubbish has been written and is being written about sailing vessels. The bulk of this tripe is perpetuated by people who have never had to hang on by their navels to an upper topsail yard in a breeze of wind.

—Weston Martyr

On Weather

For landlubbers, weather is of only passing importance unless they happen to be farmers. Cold weather is a fire in the fireplace, rain means you roll up your car windows, wind is when you hold onto your hat.

Sailors, however, are far closer to the vagaries of weather. Too much wind is just as bad as no wind. Fog can be frightening and disorienting. Storms are a test for sailors, and waves can range from sparkling summer swells that toss back a spritzing of spray to towering black mountains that threaten your very existence.

In this section you will find several quotations about Cape Horn which, to sailors, is the equivalent of Mount Everest to climbers. It is the ne plus ultra of challenges, since it has a fearsome reputation for foul weather.

Endurance is what weather teaches to sailors: endurance to survive the most savage gale as well as the glassy calm.

They were all fine sailing days, but unfortunately they were ideal only for sailing in the wrong direction.

—Francis Brenton

It is remarkable how quickly a good and favorable wind can sweep away the maddening frustrations of shore living.

—Ernest K. Gann

The profound calm which only apparently precedes and prophesies of the storm, is perhaps more awful than the storm itself; for, indeed, the calm is but the wrapper and envelope of the storm, and contains it in itself, as the seemingly harmless rifle holds the fatal powder, and the ball, and the explosion.

—HERMAN MELVILLE

Wind is to us what money is to life on shore.

—STERLING HAYDEN

I don't know who named them swells. There's nothing swell about them. They should have named them awfuls.

—HUGO VIHLEN

It is the last word in the lexicon of sailormen. There Nature has arranged trials and tribulations so ingeniously that in the van of all synonyms for sea cruelty and hardship is the ironbound name of Cape Horn. Winds blow elsewhere as strongly as they do south of fifty. Seas elsewhere may pyramid as high, break as heavily. There may be places equally remote and as bleakly lonely. Currents in other regions may be as adverse. These foes the sailorman may encounter and best, but always in his heart he will wonder if he could face all combined.

—WARWICK C. TOMPKINS

If you have never been at sea in a heavy gale, you can form no idea of the confusion of mind occasioned by the wind and spray together. They blind, deafen, and strangle you, and take away all power of action or reflection.

—EDGAR ALLAN POE

It's scary to have a 30-foot wave chasing you. If you're steering, you don't look back. The crew looks back for you, and you watch their faces. When they look straight up, get ready.

—MAGNUS OLSSON

Below fifty degrees south there is no law.
Below sixty degrees south there is no God.
> —OLD SAILOR'S SAYING

I hate storms, but calms undermine my spirits.
> —BERNARD MOITESSIER

Fog is very terrible. It comes about you before you realize and you are suddenly blind and dumb and cold.
> —ANNE MORROW LINDBERGH

I have had to pass a considerable portion of my life aboard small craft of various kinds, and after a long and mixed experience of the life, I have come to two very definite conclusions concerning it. One is that life on a small boat in fine weather is the only kind of life worth living. The other is that, in bad weather, it's just plain hell.

—WESTON MARTYR

The difference between a gale and what has become known as a "survival" storm is that in the former, with winds of force 8, or perhaps 9 (say 30 to 45 knots mean velocity), the skipper and crew retain control and can take measures which they think best, whereas in a survival gale of force 10 or over, perhaps gusting at hurricane strength, wind and sea become the masters.

—K. ADLARD COLES

Being hove to in a long gale is the most boring way of being terrified I know.

—DONALD HAMILTON

The wind and waves are always on the side of the ablest navigator.

—EDMUND GIBBON

I loved cruising the coast of Maine. For one thing, it helped me conquer my fear of fog. Not that I have learned to feel secure in the fog, but at least I have learned how to grope without panic.

—HERB PAYSON

Always sail defensively in fog, and keep in mind that you may run across people who don't know what they are doing.

—PERRY LEWIS

It is far better to spend one more lumpy, safe night at sea than to stand on in, risking your vessel and everyone aboard, just for the sake of reaching smooth water, or to be able to say you got in a day earlier.

—ROSS NORGROVE

After four days of gradually worsening weather, the Atlantic had finally erupted into violence . . .

Braced inside the cabin, I was at the mercy of the sea. There was nothing I could do against the shifting, blinding walls of water that surrounded us. They came with the sound of freight trains and broke over the boat like thunder. Again and again *Yankee Girl* reeled as if she had been hit with a giant sledgehammer.

—GERRY SPIESS

We had less snow and hail . . . but we had an abundance of what is worse to a sailor in cold weather-drenching rain. Snow is blinding, and very bad when coming upon a coast, but, for genuine discomfort, give me rain with freezing weather.

—RICHARD HENRY DANA

The approaching storm turns the surface of the sea to steel and silver. Only danger reflects clearly from such a mirror.

—HAYDEN STONE

There's no such thing as bad weather, only bad clothes.

—NORWEGIAN ADAGE

When the full displeasure of the elements falls upon a man, he is temporarily overwhelmed and permanently changed within. After the trial he is either dead or forever afterward humble and discreet.

—ERNEST K. GANN

I often sail with clever, knowledgeable folk who have one look at the sky at dawn and say: "Hmm, I don't like the look of the sky at all. We shall have more wind than we want today." The ominous signs which seem so obvious to them are usually invisible to me, so I go below and tap the glass and wonder whether they are right. But as often as not they are wrong.

—HUMPHREY BARTON

The waves rose high, but I had a good ship. Still, in the dismal fog I felt myself drifting into loneliness, an insect on a straw in the midst of the elements.

—JOSHUA SLOCUM

Off Cape Horn there are but two kinds of weather, neither one of them a pleasant kind.

—JOHN MASEFIELD

The wan and sickly daylight lasted a bare seven hours out of the twenty-four. For the rest of the time we were plunged in complete darkness, a cold, hail-smitten darkness, black as the Earl of Hell's riding boots.

—Rex Clements

For what is the array of the strongest ropes, the tallest spars, and the stoutest canvas against the mighty breath of the infinite, but thistle stalks, cobwebs, and gossamer.

—Joseph Conrad

The clouds raced with her mastheads; they rose astern enormous and white, soared to the zenith, flew past, and, falling down the wide curve of the sky, seemed to dash headlong into the sea—the clouds swifter than the ship, more free, but without a home.

—JOSEPH CONRAD

The barometer sinks, then rises, then drops; there is the same dark play in the storm. You hear the sob of creation. The sea is the great weeper. She is filled with complaint; the ocean laments for all that suffers.

—VICTOR HUGO

[We're] sailing in warm conditions with clouds coming at us like balls in a bowling alley.

—GRANT SPANHAKE

———⚫———

Now and again when we rose on the inflated crest of a glassy swell I could see the protruding end of a buoy stuck like a splinter in the flat hand of the sea.

—JOE RICHARDS

The pleasures of being becalmed had been worn threadbare; there is a limit to untutored stargazing . . .

—CHARLES LANDERY

There are numerous tortures designed especially for sailing men—perhaps to keep them humble. One is the pure physical torture of being becalmed in a rolling sea. It is worse than being in a storm and even more exhausting. And while his body cries in protest, the ship cries with him, for a sailing ship becalmed is a world of tortured noises.

—ERNEST K. GANN

I once knew a writer who, after saying beautiful things about the sea, passed through a Pacific hurricane, and he became a changed man.

—JOSHUA SLOCUM

At a quarter of two, the long-awaited-for appeared. The *Cimba* climbed a wave, and looking far to windward, I saw a black shape reared from horizon to horizon. As we dropped down a slope, I knew we were fated to meet the greatest sea I had ever come upon.

—RICHARD MAURY

A storm at sea is, I am sure, a noble spectacle. The beating of the sea upon one's face, the dashing of the waves across the deck, the spray turned into a rainbow by the sun, the quivering of the ship as trough after trough is breasted; it is all, I am very certain, very fine. But it is rather differently that I have seen it. Ignobly prostrate in my cabin, I have watched through half-seeing eyes my possessions heap themselves into chaos on the floor.

—ALEC WAUGH

Against the faintest silver of the southeastern sky an Andean ridge of black water was marching hugely in the dawn. It was one of the big seas that travel alone: a rogue elephant of the ocean. Its massive head was swaying and tossing with a leisurely deliberation that spoke imperiously to some primitive center in us. And *Wylo* was already soaring up its black precipitous face.

—FRANK WIGHTMAN

Confronting a storm is like fighting God. All the powers in the universe seem to be against you and, in an extraordinary way, your irrelevance is at the same time both humbling and exalting.

—FRANCOISE LEGRANDE

Head winds are sore vexations & the more passengers the sorer.

—RALPH WALDO EMERSON

The sea was lashed up into tremendous confusion. There was a fearful sullen sound of rushing waves and broken surges. Deep called unto deep. At times the black volume of clouds overhead seemed rent asunder by flashes of lightning, which quivered along the foaming billows, and made the succeeding darkness doubly terrible. The thunders bellowed over the wild waste of waters and were echoed and prolonged by the mountain waves. As I saw the ship staggering and plunging among these roaring caverns, it seemed miraculous that she regained her balance or preserved her buoyancy. Her yards would dip into the water; her bow was almost buried beneath the waves. Sometimes and impending surge appeared ready to overwhelm her, and nothing but a dexterous movement of the helm preserved her from the shock.

—WASHINGTON IRVING

At night, like a slumbering giant of mythology, the trade wind breathed more softly. But with the coming of the sun it heaved a sigh, rolled over, and soon assumed the deeper and more powerful breathing of a man at work.

—WILLIAM ROBINSON

On Engines

If sailors ever had a love-hate relationship, it is with their engines. Cursed when they don't work, praised when driving you through a flat calm or away from a lee shore, they are even more maligned than landlubbers.

To be fair, an engine in a sailboat is often so badly treated that, if it were a crewmember, it would jump ship immediately. Used only to get in and out of the harbor and then left idle deep in the bilge amid moisture and corrosive salt air with only a passing glance as maintenance, it's often a surprise that engines start at all.

In this section, you'll find sailors berating their engines, celebrating them, and solving their problems in many ways.

Now, motors, like women, are not all bad, but it must be admitted there is a great difference among them. I prefer the simple, clean, reliable ones, and admire the economical ones, and almost love the quiet ones that are small and don't smell, but here again we must make a compromise, as all through a yacht's design, for whereas the small ones are economical, they are apt to be hot and smelly, while the big ones keep quiet and cool.

—L. Francis Herreshoff

Long ocean passages usually don't require an engine; it's the ports and headlands at each end that may demand some expert sailing.

—Hal Roth

I used my engine for two years, and then, taking arms against a sea of troubles, cut my troubles in half by pitching *Little Dipper*'s engine overside. . . . Life afloat was vastly simplified. No more anxieties about cigarettes, drip pans, backfire baffles. No more work on spark plugs, coil, or stuffing box. A welcome reduction in yard bills. Guests forebore to make schedules, and so proved better company. When the engine went overside I began really to enjoy what I had bought a boat to get: the freedom and zest of sail.

—RICHARD BAUM

I would rather die of thirst, ten miles off the headlands in a brazen calm, having lost my dinghy in the previous storm, than have on board what is monstrously called today an "auxiliary." The name is worthy of the thing. By auxiliaries the Roman army perished. Further, it is a nasty foreign sort of term. Call it the machine and tell the truth. I am told by those who use the abomination that it is ashamed of itself, and often will not start, as though to say, "You came out to sail the seas, and I am reluctant to cheat wind, weather, and tide in your favor."

—HILAIRE BELLOC

The exhaust of *Don Quixote*'s engine was short, so it would not interfere with passage of the sail across deck and it was aimed straight up in the air. As a consequence it blew the most perfect smoke rings I have ever seen and sometimes I would start the engine in port just so visitors could admire the display.

—ERNEST K. GANN

On a breathless night there is something in the lazy drone of the motor and the undeviating wake of phosphorescent water stretching out astern that gets me almost as much as the keener joys of sailing. Every revolution of the propeller means something, and every mile puts us in a more favorable position to employ the wind when it comes in again.

—ALFRED LOOMIS

At last, the god-damned engine is silent.

 —William Snaith

On the eighth day, Sam . . . tinkered with the engine in a forlorn way, passing the time, really, while I, being of little faith, loafed and mocked. Perhaps it was the mockery and perhaps it was the ability of the others: but probably it was just cussedness that brought the engine to life with a roar. It was not a man-eating, red-blooded roar, however; just the cry of a lion turned vegetarian and very uncertain of himself.

 —Charles Landery

He was now convinced that the most valuable sail on board was the diesel.

—Ray Kauffman

—•••—

According to mythology the virtue of these engines lies in the fact that they are simple and reliable. Although this myth is widely believed, I am able to report that it is completely untrue. These engines are, in fact, vindictive, debased, black-minded ladies of no virtue and any non-Newfoundlander who goes shipmate with one is either a fool or a masochist, and is likely both.

—Farley Mowat

. . . that tin Judas down below.

—FRANK WIGHTMAN

The only reason that *Uldra*'s engine never failed was because she did not have one.

—DENNIS PULESTON

My experience with engines is that if you depend on them they fail you, but if it just doesn't matter, they serve you.

—FRANK WIGHTMAN

I can't wait for the oil wells to run dry, for the last gob of black, sticky muck to come oozing out of some remote well. Then the glory of sail will return.

—Tristan Jones

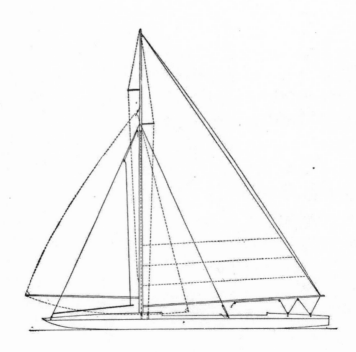

On Racing

Racing sailboats is as old as the second boat and it has gone from being commercial to being a pure sport we call "Corinthian" and back again to an increasingly commercial bent.

Years ago, harbor pilots would race their boats out to incoming ships, with the fastest pilot schooners earning the most money by being first to provide their services. Fast commercial squareriggers vied to set records in transoceanic crossings, because speed was a commodity that could be sold to customers.

There came a period when "yacht racing" was the summer sport of the very wealthy and then, with the advent of affordable boats, it became a pleasure for everyman. Today, with America's Cup yachts and Whitbread 'Round the World racers plastered with corporate logos like race cars at the Indy 500, it has once again grown a commercial edge.

But as long as there are sailboats and sailors, there will always be the challenge of racing, which is covered in this section.

When I was just learning to race, my father kept saying to me, "Son, if you want to do well in this sport, be first at the start, stay out in front, and increase your lead."

—BUDDY MELGES

———•••———

Sailboat racing becomes a game of chance only when you are not prepared.

—BUDDY MELGES

Like it's still tied to the dock!

—TED TURNER, WHEN ASKED HOW THE NEW 12-METER, *MARINER*, SAILED

We don't just want the Cup, we want the whole damn island!

—TOM BLACKALLER, ON RETRIEVING THE AMERICA'S CUP FROM AUSTRALIA

Having the Lloyd's Register of Shipping certify these America's Cup racers is a bit like having the Royal English Trucking Association certify a Formula One race car.

—TOM BLACKALLER

Learning how to make a boat go fast is easier ashore than it is afloat because there is no time to stop and think when you are racing.

—PAUL ELVSTROM

———•:••:•———

Paul Cayard: They're not even covering us anymore. Tom Whidden: I don't think they're even looking back!

———•:••:•———

Sailing is a good sport. You don't have to beat up the other guy like you do in boxing or football; you just try to outsmart him, and outsail him, and then you go out and have a beer with him.

—JOHN KOLIUS

The chance for mistakes is about equal to the number of crew squared.

—TED TURNER

If she is right, then we are all wrong.

—MARQUIS OF ANGLESEY ABOUT THE YACHT *AMERICA*, 1851

Where else in the sporting world would the press proclaim as "Grand Prix Racing" the sorry spectacle of twelve men slumped over a wet rail, slogging along at eight knots on a $200,000 object that is obsolete the next season?

—GARRY HOYT

There's one rich man on board and there's twenty-five poor men and they enjoy it more than the rich man does.

—JIM KILROY, WHEN ASKED IF YACHT RACING IS A RICH MAN'S SPORT

————

I have sailed with and against the best in 12-meters, ocean racers and small boats, and I think I have learned something from each person. What is interesting is that although each is especially good at one particular thing—leadership, boat preparation, helmsmanship—they all have this in common: when they get up in the morning and look at themselves in the mirror, they all have the self-confidence to be able to say realistically, "I'm the best."

—DENNIS CONNER

The United States, this once-great nation and land of the free, is chicken-hearted. The American emblem, the bald eagle, should be changed to a spastic canary. The decision smacks of 300 million people in the most technologically advanced place in the world being dead scared of three million sheep farmers.

—BEN LEXCEN

———

This is no democracy. However, I do like to hear any well thought out, reasonable suggestion. Once.

—BUS MOSBACHER

The wood ain't growing yet that'll beat *Bluenose*.

—CAPT. ANGUS WALTERS

———— ❦ ————

Protesting the New York Yacht Club is like complaining about your wife to your mother-in-law.

—SIR FRANK PACKER

The virtues of the discomfort of an ocean-racing yacht—wet clothes, lack of sleep, bunk sharing and the constant pressure to outrace frequently invisible competitors—are difficult to explain yet addictive. For the men and women who keep returning to the Fastnet and other long-distance races until they are on the verge of old age, the lure is not the hope of winning trophies. Perhaps the sport provides a means of rediscovering some lost part of their primitive nature, unsullied by civilized life.

—JOHN ROUSMANIERE

The quality that links all of these sailors (and myself) is a winning self-image. They know they are the best men for the job of winning sailboat races, and most of them keep looking for more sailboat races to win. They have the self-confidence to know when to ask for help from experts and to know that playing the percentages is better than taking chances. They are talented, competitive men but intelligent enough to realize that skill and drive are not enough. They have to work hard too.

I think it all comes down to a statement: "Give yourself no excuse to lose."

—DENNIS CONNER

Many people develop a kind of love-hate relationship with the spinnaker, and it has often been said that this sail is the easiest to hoist but requires the most courage.

—R. "BUNTY" KING

There might be some doubt about his ability to win the cup, but no doubt about his ability to capture our hearts.

—MAYOR JIMMY WALKER

Ocean racing is made up of many bad afternoons, ugly mornings, and hard nights.

—WILLIAM SNAITH

What do you say to this? Let everyone send a dollar apiece for a fund to buy a loving cup for Sir Thomas Lipton bigger than the one he would have got if he won, contributed to by everybody that really admires a fine sportsman. Send it to, I will suggest, a Lipton Cup Fund—care of Mayor Walker in New York. Let Jimmy buy it and present it on behalf of everybody with an inscription along this line: "To possibly the world's worst yacht builder but absolutely the world's most cheerful loser." You have been a benefit to mankind. Sir Thomas, you have made losing worthwhile.

—WILL ROGERS, IN A LETTER TO THE *NEW YORK TIMES* AFTER LIPTON LOST THE AMERICA'S CUP

The boat is hitting 24 knots as I write this to you and the term "the decks are awash" does not do justice to what is going on out here. The water is rushing around like a flooding river. When I came down below just now my cheeks were bruised from being pelted in the face by ice water for five hours.

—PAUL CAYARD

It's like standing under a cold shower tearing up five-pound notes.

—PRIME MINISTER OF ENGLAND, TED HEATH, ABOUT OCEAN RACING

We won the race by twenty-three seconds, and two seconds after we had crossed the line the mast snapped. Which solved the problem of stopping, anyway.

—PHILIP HOLLAND

To the electric excitement when pored-over plans and dull days of practice somehow come together in a racing move that shakes you free of the pack; . . . you cross the fleet and taste the sudden silence and splendid loneliness of first place.

—GARRY HOYT

I have no intention of giving up hope that some day I may have a yacht that will beat my American friends and thus realize my lifelong ambition.

—Sir Thomas Lipton

I can't win. I can't win.

—Sir Thomas Lipton

I've won America's Cup races by one second. That's where I come from, feet and inches, seconds. In that environment, you don't give up anything to anyone.

—PAUL CAYARD

———

The America's Cup is a race of management, money, technology, teamwork and, last and incidentally, sailing.

—BILL KOCH

On Philosophy

For centuries, philosophers, poets, and writers have used the sea and sailors as allegorical images to convey ideas and emotions. The endless sea, the restless sea, the enduring sea—it's sometimes hard to get away from the sea when it seems to pour from every book.

The same is true of sailors and their arts. Beating into the wind is always symbolic of man's struggle, running free is equated with times of pleasure. Our tiny boats carry us on voyages that are like the course of our lives, and we always reach that final anchorage.

In this section, you'll find a gathering of this philosophical approach to sailing and the sea, often by writers who may never have ventured past the breakwater.

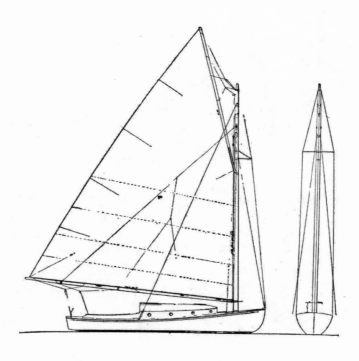

Let your boat of life be light, packed with only what you need: a homely home and simple pleasures, one or two friends, worth the name, someone to love and someone to love you, a cat, a dog, and a pipe or two, enough to eat and enough to wear, and a little more than enough to drink; for thirst is a dangerous thing.

—JEROME K. JEROME

for whatever we lose (like a you or a me)
it's always ourselves we find in the sea.

—E.E. CUMMINGS

So we beat on against the current, borne back ceaselessly into the past.

—F. Scott Fitzgerald

Anyone can hold the helm when the sea is calm.

—Syrus Publilius

In sailing, as in life, momentum is a valued commodity, the secondary source of power that keeps us going long after the original source has disappeared.

—Richard Bode

The sail, the play of its pulse so like our own lives: so thin and yet so full of life, so noiseless when it labors hardest, so noisy and impatient when least effective.

—HENRY DAVID THOREAU

A community is like a ship; everyone ought to be prepared to take the helm.

—HENRIK IBSEN

The way of a boat skimming the water, how free she runs. She is free only when you have let her fall off again and have recovered once more her nice adjustment to the forces she must obey and cannot defy.

—WOODROW WILSON

There must be more to sailing than the mere setting out to sail from A to B via C. There must be exploration, not only of new areas of the ocean, but also of new parts of yourself.

—TRISTAN JONES

Thought is the wind, knowledge the sail, and mankind the vessel.
—AUGUST HARE

Ideals are like stars. You will not succeed in touching them with your hands, but like the seafaring man on the ocean desert of waters, you choose them as your guides, and following them, you reach your destiny.
—CARL SCHURZ

And men go forth, and admire lofty mountains and broad seas, and roaring torrents, and the course of the stars, and forget their own selves in doing so.

—PETRARCH

If a man does not know to what port he is steering, no wind is favorable to him.

—SENECA

No pessimist ever discovered the secret of the stars, or sailed to an uncharted land, or opened a new doorway for the human spirit.

—HELEN KELLER

⸻

He that will not sail till all dangers are over must never put to sea.

—THOMAS FULLER

Life hangs on a very thin thread and the cancer of time is complacency. If you are going to do something, do it now. Tomorrow is too late.

—PETE GOSS

The pessimist complains about the wind; the optimist expects it to change; the realist adjusts the sails.

—WILLIAM ARTHUR WARD

Revenge and deep water have much in common. A man may get sucked down into either and drown before he understands the true danger.

—HAYDEN STONE

———•×•×•———

I find the great thing in this world is not so much where we stand, as in what direction we are moving; to reach the port of heaven, we must sail sometimes with the wind and sometimes against it—but we must sail, and not drift, nor lie at anchor.

—OLIVER WENDELL HOLMES

Indeed, the cruising of a boat here and there is very much what happens to the soul of man in a larger way. We set out for places which we do not reach, or reach too late; and, on the way, there befall us all manner of things which we could never have awaited.

—HILAIRE BELLOC

Ｆor the truth is that I already know as much about my fate as I need to know. The day will come when I will die. So the only matter of consequence before me is what I will do with my allotted time. I can remain on shore, paralyzed with fear, or I can raise my sails and dip and soar in the breeze.

—RICHARD BODE

Works and Authors Cited

Adams, John, second U.S. President

Anderson, J.R.L., British mystery writer in *The Guardian* newspaper

Ashley, Clifford, author *Ashley's Book of Knots*

Atkin, William, naval architect

Ballard, Robert, adventurer and discoverer of Titanic

Bardinaux, Marcel, author, *The Four Winds of Adventure*

Barton, Humphrey, author, *Westward Crossing, Vertue XXXV* (1952)

Baum, Richard, author, *By the Wind*

Belloc, Hilaire, author, *On Sailing the Sea*

Bertrand, John, Australian skipper of winning America's Cup yacht, 1983, author, *Born to Win*

Beston, Henry, author, *The Outermost House*

Blackaller, Tom, America's Cup skipper

Bloomfield, Howard, author, *Sailing to the Sun*

Bode, Richard, author, *First You Have to Row a Little Boat*

Borland, Loren R., author, *Shipshape and Bristol Fashion*

Brenton, Francis, author, *Long Sail to Haiti, Voyage of the Sierra Sagrada*

Brown, Alan, author, *Invitation to Sailing*

Buckley Jr., William F., author, *Racing Through Paradise*

Buffett, Jimmy, singer, author, *A Pirate Looks at 50*

Burke, Edmund, author, *On the Sublime and Beautiful*

Callahan, H. A., author, *Learning to Sail*

Carnegie, Dale, motivational lecturer

Carson, Rachel, scientist, author, *The Sea Around Us*

Cayard, Paul, America's Cup and Whitbread skipper

Chichester, Sir Francis, 'round the world sailor, author, *Gipsy Moth Circles the World*

Childers, Erskine, Irish revolutionary, author, *Riddle of the Sands*

Chiles, Webb, adventurer/author, *Storm Passage*

Clements, Rex, author, *A Gipsy of the Horn*

Coles, K. Adlard, author, *Heavy Weather Sailing*

Conner, Dennis, America's Cup winner, author, *Comeback, No Excuse to Lose*

Conrad, Joseph, author, *Mirror of the Sea, Nigger of the Narcissus, Lord Jim, Typhoon*

Cooper, James Fenimore, author, *The Pilot*

Cornell, Gwenda, author, *Pacific Odyssey*

Crane, Stephen, author, *The Open Boat*

Culler, R.D. (Pete), boat designer/builder

cummings, e.e., poet, "the sea"

Dana, Richard Henry, author, *Two Years Before the Mast*

Davis, Charles G., nautical historian

Davison, Ann, author, *My Ship Is So Small*

Day, George, author, *Sailing in Thin Water*

Day, Thomas Fleming—First editor of *Rudder* magazine

Degnon, Dom, author, *Sails Full & By*

de Hartog, Jan, offshore sailor

Depue, Anne, author, *I'd Rather be Sailing*

Dinesen, Isak, author, *Out of Africa*

Dodd, Edward, author, *Great Dipper to Southern Cross*

Doyle, Sir Arthur Conan, author, *Adventure of Abbey Grange*

Drake, Sir Francis, explorer, *Letters*

Duke of Wellington, British general who defeated Napoleon at Waterloo.

Dumas, Vito, cruising sailor, author, *Alone Through the Roaring Forties*

Emerson, Ralph Waldo, philosopher and essayist

Elvstrom, Paul, championship sailor

Fielding, Henry, novelist/dramatist

Fitzgerald, F. Scott, author, *The Great Gatsby*

Flynn, Errol, actor, *Captain Blood* (1935)

Fowles, John, author, *Shipwreck*

Fox, Uffa, racing sailor/author, *According to Uffa*

Francis, Clare, British novelist and long-distance sailor, author, *Come Hell or High Water*

Gann, Ernest K., pilot, sailor, author, *Song of the Sirens*

Gerbault, Alain, cruising sailor, author, *The Fight of the Firecrest*

Gibbon, Edmund, historian, *Decline and Fall of the Roman Empire*

Gibbons, Thomas, author, *Boxing the Compass*

Goldberg, Whoopi, actress

Goss, Pete, 'round the world skipper, author, *Close to the Wind*

Gossett Jr., Lou, actor

Graham, Robin Lee, circumnavigator, author, *Dove*

Greenhill, Basil, author, *Sailing for a Living*

Griffiths, Maurice, author, *Swatchways and Little Ships*

Gustafson, Chuck, author, *How to Buy the Best Sailboat*

Hamilton, Donald, sailor, author of Matt Helm adventure books

Hanna, John G., yacht designer

Hardy, Sir James, Australian America's Cup skipper

Hayden, Sterling, sailor, actor, author, *Wanderer*

Heath, Ted, former British Prime Minister, sailor, author, *On Sailboat Racing*

Herreshoff, L. Francis, yacht designer, *The Compleat Cruiser*, *Sensible Cruising Designs*

Herreshoff, Nathanael G., yacht designer

Hersey, John, author, *A Single Pebble*

Heyerdahl, Thor, explorer/author, *Kon-Tiki*

Hiscock, Eric, circumnavigator

Holdridge, Desmond, author, *Northern Lights*

Holland, Philip, contributor, *The Yachtsman* magazine

Holmes, Oliver Wendell, judge, author, *The Autocrat at the Breakfast Table*

Homer, author, *The Odyssey*

Hoyt, Garry, designer, author, *Go for the Gold*

Hugo, Victor, author, *Toilers of the Sea*

Ibsen, Henrik, playwright

Innes, Hammond, adventure author

Irving, Washington, author, *Sketch Book of Geoffrey Crayon, Gent.*

James, Naomi, 'round the world sailor

Janovy, John Jr., author, *Back in Keith County*

Jerome, Jerome K., author, *Three Men in a Boat*

Johnson, Dr. Samuel, author

Jones, Ted, author, *The Offshore Racer*

Jones, Tristan, cruising sailor, author, *Yarns, Ice*

Kauffman, Ray, author, *Hurricane's Wake*

Keller, Helen, blind activist, author

Kennedy, John F., U.S. President and sailor

Kilroy, Jim, owner of *Kialoa*

King, R. "Bunty," author, *Spinnaker*

Kinney, Francis, yacht designer, author, *Skene's Elements of Yacht Design*

Kipling, Rudyard, poet

Koch, Bill, America's Cup winner

Kolius, John, America's Cup skipper

Landery, Charles, author, *Whistling for a Wind*

Legrande, Francoise, author, *Boatopia*

Lethbridge, T. C., author

Lewis, Perry, author

Lexcen, Ben, Australian yacht designer

Lindbergh, Anne Morrow, author, *Hour of Gold, Hour of Lead*

Lipton, Sir Thomas, British tea magnate and America's Cup competitor

Lipton, Sir Thomas

London, Jack, author

Long, Dwight, author, *Sailing All Seas in the Idle Hour*

Loomis, Alfred, editor of *Yachting* magazine

Luther, Martin, author

MacGregor, John, author, *The Voyage Alone in the Yawl Rob Roy*

Mannix, RAdm. Daniel III, naval officer, author, *The Old Navy*

Manry, Robert, author, *Tinkerbelle*

Martyr, Weston, author, *The Southseaman*

Masefield, John, poet laureate of England, "A Tarpaulin Muster," "Bird of Dawning," "Sea Fever"

Maury, Richard, author, *Saga of Cimba*

Melges, Buddy, racing sailor, author, *Sailing Smart*

Melville, Herman, author, *Moby-Dick, White Jacket, Typee*

Mitchell, Carleton, author, *Passage East*

Moitessier, Bernard, author, *The Long Way*

Monsarrat, Nicholas, author

Montalban, Ricardo, actor

Montgomery, Roselle Mercier, author

Morison, Samuel Eliot, historian, author, *Spring Tides*

Mosbacher, Bus, America's Cup skipper 1962

Mowat, Farley, author, *The Boat Who Wouldn't Float*

Mull, Gary, yacht designer

Nimitz, Adm. Chester, retired WWII leader

Norgrove, Ross, author

Olsson, Magnus, Whitbread sailor

O'Neill, Eugene, playwright, *Long Day's Journey into Night, Mourning Becomes Electra*

Packer, Sir Frank, America's Cup challenger

Palley, Reese, cruising sailor, author, *There Be No Dragons, Unlikely Passages*

Pardey, Lin and Larry, cruising sailors/authors

Payson, Herb, author

Pidgeon, Harry, cruising sailor

Pitkin, James S., sailor

Poe, Edgar Allan, author, *Descent into a Maelstrom*

Puleston, Dennis, author, *Blue Water Vagabond*

Pye, E. A., author, *Red Mains'l*

Raleigh, Sir Walter, adventurer

Ransome, Arthur, author, *Racundra's First Cruise*, *The Big Six*

Reeman, Douglas, British adventure and nautical novelist

Richards, Professor E. J., British professor of yacht design

Richards, Joe, author, *Princess*

Robinson, William, author, *Ten Thousand Leagues Over the Sea*, *To the Great Southern Sea*

Rogers, Will, letter to *New York Times*

Rose, Robert N, author, *My Ship O' Dreams*

Roth, Hal, author, *Two Against Cape Horn*

Rothrock, Bill, author, *The Long Distance Cruiser*

Rousmaniere, John, author

Sainte-Exupery, Antoine de, pilot, sailor, author

Sayers, Dorothy, mystery author, *Nine Tailors*

Seidman, David, author, *The Complete Sailor*

Seneca, Roman poet and philosopher

Slocum, Joshua, author, *Sailing Alone Around the World*

Smith, Hervey Garrett, author, *The Arts of the Sailor*

Snaith, William, author, *On the Winds Way*

Spanhake, Grant—Chessie Whitbreak '97

Spiess, Gerry, singlehanded sailor, lost at sea

Steinbeck, John, author and Nobel Prize winner, *Sea of Cortez*

Stephens, Roderick, naval architect

Stevenson, Robert Louis, author, *An Inland Voyage*

Stokes, Francis, American singlehanded sailor

Stone, Hayden, On the Way of Water

Synge, John, playwright

Syrus, Publilius, first century Roman writer

Thoreau, Henry David, philosopher and author

Thurber, James, humorist

Tolkien, J.R.R., author, *The Fellowship of the Ring*

Tomlinson, H. M., journalist and novelist

Tompkins, Warwick C., sailor

Trent, Buzzy, surfer

Turner, Ted, billionaire America's Cup skipper

Twain, Mark, humorist

Ullman, Liv, actress

Van De Wiele, Annie, round-the-world sailor

Vihlen, Hugo, sailor

Villiers, Alan, sailor, author, *Cruise of the Conrad*

Violet, Charles, author, *Solitary Journey*

Walker, Mayor Jimmy, flamboyant New York C ity mayor

Walters, Capt. Angus, skipper of *Bluenose*

Waugh, Alec, author, *Hot Countries*

Whidden, Tom, America's Cup sailor and North Sails president

White, E. B., author, *The Sea and the Wind That Blows*

White, Joel, author, *Woodenboat Mag*

Whitman, Walt, poet, author, *The Beauty of the Ship*

Wicker, Tom, journalist

Wightman, Frank, author, *Wylo Sails Again*

Wilson, Woodrow, 28th U.S. President

Notes on Selected Authors

Humphrey Barton sailed from England to New York double-handed in a Vertue class 25-ft. sloop and wrote about it in *Vertue XXXV* (1952).

Richard Baum sailed a lovely W. Starling Burgess–designed cutter, *Little Dipper*, along the Eastern U.S. and into the Caribbean, which he recounted in *By the Wind* (1962).

Tom Blackaller was an irrepressible racing sailor with an impressive record in Stars when he became involved in the America's Cup, where he was one of the most colorful characters.

Jimmy Buffett is arguably the singer laureate of sailors everywhere, and his songs are standard fare aboard sailboat stereos everywhere. I will break your heart by telling you that his success has allowed him to buy . . . a powerboat!

Rachel Carson was an American writer and ocean environmentalist whose *The Sea Around Us* set the standard for ecological concerns.

Paul Cayard is a San Francisco–based sailor who has carved a reputation in everything from Lasers to America's Cup Yachts to the Whitbread 'Round the World Race, which he won.

Francis Chichester was an amazing single-hander who sailed and wrote about a series of Gipsy Moths. *Atlantic Adventure* (1963), *Romantic Challenge* (1972).

K. Adlard Coles, a well-known sailor and publisher of English marine books, wrote *Heavy Weather Sailing*, a treatise on offshore sailing that remains the leading reference to this day.

Dennis Conner is arguably the best-known racing sailor in the world, thanks to his skill in sailing America's Cup yachts. He has been credited—and blamed—with changing the face of America's Cup racing and is the first person to both lose the America's Cup (1983) and win it back (1987).

Joseph Conrad was an English novelist and longtime mariner.

Richard Henry Dana was an American sailor who wrote *Two Years Before the Mast*.

Ann Davison made a single-handed transatlantic crossing in *Felicity Ann*, a 23-ft. double-ended sloop, and wrote about it in *My Ship Is So Small* (1956).

Thomas Fleming Day was the editor of *The Rudder* and a champion of ocean voyaging in small boats long before it was commonplace, writing *Across the Atlantic in Sea Bird* in 1911.

Isak Dinesen is a Danish writer best known as the author of *Out of Africa* (1937).

Vito Dumas was an Argentinian single-handed sailor who was the first to sail around the world via Cape Horn east to west.

Paul Elvstrom has been called "The Great Dane" for his championship racing skills, holding the record for having won more Olympic gold medals (four) than any sailor.

Ernest K. Gann was an American pilot, sailor, and author who chronicled his sailing adventures in *Song of the Sirens* and his flying tales in books such as *The High & The Mighty*.

Alain Gerbault was a dramatic Frenchman who did a westbound circumnavigation in a 39-ft. cutter, *Firecrest*, and wrote about it in two books.

Pete Goss is a 'Round the World single-handed racer who gripped the fascination of the world by his rescue against great odds of another racer who capsized in the Southern Ocean.

Robin Lee Graham captured the imagination of America when, as a 16-year-old, he sailed around the world in *Dove*, a 24-ft. sloop and wrote about it in *National Geographic*. He finished the voyage aboard a 33-ft. sloop, married, and moved inland.

Kenneth Grahame's *The Wind in the Willows* has delighted generations of children (and adults) with tales of Toad, Mole, and Water Rat.

Maurice Griffiths wrote about the pleasures of cruising around England in *Swatchways and Little Ships* (1971), which covered everything from a lifetime of stories to boat design.

Sterling Hayden was discovered by Hollywood aboard a Down East schooner and his blond good looks made him an immediate star. His real love was the sea, about which he wrote in *Wanderer*.

Ted Heath is an ocean racing sailor as well as the former Prime Minister of England.

L. Francis Herreshoff was a well-known American naval architect.

Nathanael Herreshoff was known as the Wizard of Bristol for his innovative designs, including six America's Cup winners.

Eric Hiscock was half of the famous husband-wife team of Eric and Susan Hiscock who circumnavigated in a 30' sloop, *Wanderer III*. Their books include *Around the World In Wanderer III* (1956), *Atlantic Cruise in Wanderer III* (1968), *Sou'West in Wanderer IV* (1973).

Garry Hoyt is a championship dinghy sailor who later produced the Freedom series of cruising yachts with unstayed masts, and whose *Go For The Gold* (1971) was a fresh look at yacht racing.

Hammond Innes was a Scottish thriller writer, sailor and travel writer. Most of his stories involved the sea, such as "The Wreck of the Mary Deare."

Tristan Jones was a quirky and charismatic English sailor and prolific author, who gained a following with his no-nonsense cruising books.

John Fitzgerald Kennedy is most remembered as President of the U.S., but he was also an avid sailor his entire life.

Sir Thomas Lipton was not only the founder of Lipton's Tea, but also a perpetually unsuccessful but exceedingly gracious challenger for the America's Cup who won the heart of America and sold them lots of tea, too.

Jack London needs little introduction as an author, and his *Cruise of the Snark* about sailing from San Francisco to Australia on a 55' ketch remains a classic of yachting.

Alfred Loomis was Alf to his friends and Spun Yarn to readers of his long-time column in Yachting Magazine that poked fun at pomp and celebrated traditional sailing values. His *Cruise of the Hippocampus* (1922) is an amusing tale of sailing from New York to Panama on a 28' yawl.

John MacGregor was a proponent of small-boat cruising, and his voyage across the English Channel in a 21-ft. canoe yawl was published as *The Voyage Alone in the Yawl Rob Roy* (1867).

Robert Manry decked over a 13½-ft Old Town skiff and sailed her from Falmouth, Mass. to Falmouth, England. Though it seemed a stunt, this single-handed voyage was actually a model of common sense and set a record at the time for the smallest sailboat to make the voyage.

John Masefield was an English sailor who was also poet laureate of England, producing sailing classics such as *Sea Fever*.

Richard Maury sailed *Cimba*, a 35-ft. Bluenose schooner, from Nova Scotia to Fiji, and wrote about it in *The Saga of Cimba* (1939).

Buddy Melges is a champion sailor and boat builder from Zenda, Wisconsin. who has sailed everything from Olympic classes (a Gold Medal) to America's Cup yachts.

Herman Melville was an American sailor/author whose best-known work was *Moby Dick* (1851).

Bernard Moitessier circumnavigated via Cape Horn in a 40-ft steel ketch named *Joshua* after his hero, Joshua Slocum.

Samuel Eliot Morison was a U.S. naval officer and nautical historian.

Bus Mosbacher skippered Weatherly in 1962 to win the America's Cup.

Gary Mull was a talented yacht designer of everything from production racers to America's Cup challengers, and a long-time friend and crew for Tom Blackaller.

Harry Pidgeon, a non-sailor when he built his enlarged version of the Sea Bird and named it *Islander*, sailed west around the world from Los Angeles, telling the story in *Around the World Single-Handed* (1933).

Dennis Puleston spent six years cruising the world aboard a series of schooners and the yawl *Uldra*, writing *Blue Water Vagabond* in 1946.

E. A. Pye and his wife sailed from England to the West Indies on their traditional English cutter, *Moonraker*, writing about it in *Red Mains'l* (1952).

Arthur Ransome is the English author of the "Swallows and Amazons" children's story, who sailed the Baltic aboard his 30-ft. double-ended ketch, *Racundra*.

Joe Richards had a long love affair with his 26-ft Friendship sloop, *Princess*, in which he sailed the East Coast. He later rebuilt the boat and sailed her to Bimini.

William Albert Robinson sailed around the world westbound from New York in his 32-ft. Alden ketch *Svaap*, only to have her confiscated by Ecuador. Later he made an 11-month, 15,000-mile cruise from Tahiti to South America and back aboard his 70-ft brigantine schooner *Varua*.

Will Rogers was not a sailor but, like many Americans, he was so taken by Sir Thomas Lipton's America's Cup sportsmanship that he wrote the quoted letter to the New York Times, which raised money to buy a cup for Lipton, who vowed to return to try again for the America's Cup.

Hal Roth and his wife sailed their 35-ft sloop, Whisper from San Francisco to Japan and back, writing about it in *Two On A Big Ocean* (1972).

John Rousmaniere is a highly respected sailor/writer whose books include *The Annapolis Book of Seamanship* and *Fastnet, Force 10*.

Dorothy Sayers remains one of the most popular British mystery authors.

Joshua Slocum is perhaps the best-known circumnavigator and certainly led many others to cruising with his *Sailing Alone Around The World* (1899).

Gerry Spiess was a sailor/writer/adventurer who made transoceanic single-handed passages aboard tiny sailboats, finally disappearing in the Pacific Ocean.

John Steinbeck was not a sailor as such, but his cruise of the Gulf of California with marine biologist Ed Ricketts (later immortalized as

Doc Ricketts in Cannery Row) captured the flavor of cruising in his book, *Sea of Cortez*.

Roderick Stephens was a racing sailor as well as half of the brother duo that founded the prestigious Sparkman & Stephens design firm.

Warwick M. Tompkins sailed the classic North Sea pilot schooner *Wander Bird* across the Atlantic, around Cape Horn and north of San Francisco, with a crew that included Irving Johnson and Tompkins son, Commodore, who went on to become a famous sailor as well.

Ted Turner, tagged "the mouth of the South" for his outspoken ways, was an America's Cup winner long before he became the billionaire founder of CNN.

Hugo Vihlin set a record for the smallest boat, at 5'3", to cross the Atlantic in 1992.

Alan Villiers was an Australian seaman/adventurer who apprenticed in the last days of sail and went on to skipper many vessels such as the square-rigger *Joseph Conrad* around the world. He wrote about it in *Cruise of the Conrad*, (1945).

Charles Violet wrote *Solitary Journey* about his voyage from England to Malta and then back via the French inland waterways aboard his 20-ft. yawl, *Nova Espero*, on which he's sailed transatlantic twice.

Index